Make It Simpler
PAPER PIECING

Easy as 1 · 2 · 3 ~ A Pinless Fold & Sew Technique

Anita Grossman Solomon

C&T PUBLISHING

Text and Artwork © 2003 Anita Grossman Solomon
Artwork © 2003 C&T Publishing
Editor-in-Chief: Darra Williamson
Editor: Jan Grigsby
Technical Editors: Katrina Lamken, Joyce Engels Lytle, Elin Thomas
Copyeditor/Proofreader: Eleanor Levie, Stacy Chamness
Cover Designer: Christina D. Jarumay
Design Director/Book Designer: Christina D. Jarumay
Illustrator: John Heisch
Production Assistant: Luke Mulks, Matt Allen, Kirstie L. McCormick
Photography: Blocks, Luke Mulks; Other quilt photography D. James Dee
unless otherwise noted; 1718 silk patchwork©The Quilters' Guild of the British
Isles; How-to photography, Diane Pedersen
Published by C&T Publishing, Inc., P.O. Box 1456, Lafayette, California, 94549

Front cover: *Jan's Star*, Anita Grossman Solomon

Library of Congress Cataloging-in-Publication Data
Solomon, Anita Grossman.
  Make it simpler paper piecing : easy as 1-2-3 a pinless fold and sew
technique / Anita Grossman Solomon.
      p. cm.
Includes index.
  ISBN 1-57120-222-6 (Paper trade)
  1. Patchwork--Patterns. 2. Quilting. I. Title.
  TT835.S629 2003
  746.46--dc21
                            2003012

Printed in China
10 9 8 7 6 5 4 3 2 1

DEDICATION

For HHS
with affection
from every fiber of my being

ACKNOWLEDGMENTS

From coast to coast, hands and hearts reached out to help me to get from start to finish, along the way transforming the creation of this book into a "virtual" quilting bee of the electronic age. Georgette Hasiotis, my college roommate, together with friends Sylvia Hughes, alter-ego Susan Stauber, and editor extraordinaire Jan Grigsby, were my respective counsel, instigator, facilitator, and mind reader.

Without the generous assistance of the following: Lisa Aswad, Patricia Cox Crews, Carolyn Ducey, Kay Fenlason, Dorothea Hahn, Marin Hanson, Laurel Horton, Cathy Izzo, Claudia Jaffe, Athena Lemakis, Suzanne Lemakis, Bridget Long, Penny McMorris, Tina Fenwick Smith, Norma Torres, the Riverbank State Park Quilters and the quilters listed and shown in the back of this book, this endeavor would be far less complete.

Simple thanks to The Electric Quilt Company, without which I wouldn't be where I am or who I have become.

These companies and their representatives were generous in providing their time and products:

Gail Kessler, Andover Fabrics, NY, NY
Karen Junquet, Chanteclaire Fabrics, NY, NY
Comic Book Legal Defense Fund, Northhampton, MA
Michele Hirschberg, Clairmont-Nichols Opticians, NY, NY
Mary Gay Leahy, Fairfield Processing Corp, Danbury, CT
Jamie Arcuri and Donna Wilder, FreeSpirit Fabrics, NY, NY
Lisa Shepard, Marcus Brothers Textiles Incorporated, NY, NY
Karen Miller and Michael Steiner, Michael Miller Fabrics, NY, NY
Julie Scribner, P&B Textiles, Burlingame, CA
Karen Diehl, Prym-Dritz Corporation, Spartanburg, SC
Demetria Zahoudanis, RJR Fabrics, Torrance, CA

My devoted husband, Horace, accommodates and encourages my interests, whether personal or professional. He was the first to realize that my interest in quilts transcends all boundaries. His steadfast support of my quilt work and for this first book has helped to transform my dreams into reality.

Anita Grossman Solomon

TABLE OF CONTENTS

E N T S

Paper, Patchwork, and the Role of Innovation

Laurel Horton

When Anita Grossman Solomon told me that her new book would introduce "the latest development in paper piecing since the nineteenth century," she got my attention. She and I are interested in some of the new discoveries in quiltmaking that may not be so "new" after all. I will share some of my thoughts about how we think about what's old and what's new.

We quilters continually see ourselves in relation to the past, whether we are aware of it or not. For many of us, one of the appeals of quiltmaking is the perceived emotional connection with our ancestors. We feel that we are re-enacting the "pioneer values" of the past; that, in the midst of our busy lives, we make the time and space to participate in a traditional activity. The quilts we make are tangible, visible proof of our connection with the past.

For others of us, quiltmaking provides opportunities to do something new and different. We feel impatient with what we perceive as the limitations imposed by the traditions we've inherited when we look at historic quilts. The past is the benchmark by which we measure our creativity and inventiveness. We are most influenced by tradition and innovation, both of which define us in terms of what has come before.

Ironically, we don't really understand the past. While we may be able to recall or recite historical facts, at the same time, we hold onto a deeper, mythological image of the lives of our ancestors. We imagine that at some point in the pre-industrial past, there was a time when people lived simple, uncomplicated lives, crafted household items by hand, helped their neighbors, and generally were better, more spiritual human beings. Quiltmaking becomes a way for us to try to recapture what we perceive to have lost.

When we visit historic sites, we may be appalled at the conditions under which our ancestors lived—the absence of privacy, and the complicated processes required to provide the basics of food, clothing, light, heat, and hot water. We come away with a perspective of history as progress, as a process of evolution. This process has brought us from the primitive state of our ancestors to our present level of success in the modern world. We feel fortunate to have our modern tools and materials as well as the intellectual and social freedom to use them. We make quilts in new, innovative styles to express the contrast between our lives and those of our ancestors.

Although we understand some of the historical trends and fashions that have influenced quiltmaking, we tend to make the biggest leaps when we interpret a quiltmaker's motivations and design choices. I remember a conversation I overheard in 1976 while I was taking notes on quilts displayed in a small historical museum. A volunteer guide was talking with a visitor about a highly ornamental crazy quilt on display, and the visitor mused "I wonder why she used all those silks and velvets? They haven't held up very well." The guide replied, "I don't know. I guess it was all she had." Even though I was just beginning my research at that point, I recognized first that the guide's interpretation was incorrect for that particular quilt, and second that her statement was based on the widely held assumption that all quilts of past generations were motivated by necessity and utility.

We have this image of our ancestors patching together the tiniest bits of fabric to make quilts in order to keep their families from freezing. This serves both the romanticized model of our ancestors as thrifty and resourceful survivors, and the evolutionary model of our ancestors as poor, primitive, and deprived of the basics that we now take for granted. This notion gets in our way a lot.

Research over the past quarter-century indicates that the earliest American quilts were created by well-to-do women. They used expensive imported fabrics to make elegant and finely crafted bedcovers. Early quilts were associated with luxury and refinement, not poverty or thrift. Poor people were more likely to use blankets, furs (in frontier settlements), or additional layers of clothing to keep warm while sleeping. This revised image of early quiltmaking deals a blow to both the romantic model of the resourcefulness of our sturdy ancestors and the evolutionary model of our progress from the primitive to the modern world.

Existing evidence suggests that, although fabric was relatively expensive, people who could afford it used it to make quilts, not just from remnants but from yardage purchased for that purpose. Further, quiltmakers did not seem to hold onto a limited range of accepted patterns or techniques. Examination of surviving bedcovers reveals that these practitioners, not unlike contemporary quiltmakers, explored a wide range of experimental and innovative techniques, singly and in combination.

With this in mind, perhaps it is not such a shock to realize that one of the major patchwork innovations of the late twentieth century—piecing by sewing fabric on paper—has historical roots. The use of paper to provide a rigid, yet flexible, backing for patchwork has been used for perhaps three centuries.

The earliest known example of patchwork in the world is "the 1718 coverlet," owned by the Quilter's Guild of the British Isles, shown below.

Constructed in geometric blocks around a larger central star motif, the individual shapes are cut from silk and pieced on paper. This technique is known as English paper template piecing, or mosaic patchwork. Unlike the more familiar repetitious hexagon and diamond shapes, the individual motifs in the 1718 coverlet include hearts, tulips, and swans.

The Pennocks, a Quaker family from Chester County, Pennsylvania, created the only currently identifiable

American example of this complex form of template work. The unquilted patchwork piece is called "the Primitive Hall quilt top," after the Pennock family home, and is inscribed with the date 1842. It is made up of twenty-five individual blocks, each pieced over paper in a different geometrical design using printed cotton fabrics.

These blocks are rare and unusual examples of an elaborate form of mosaic patchwork. This technique enjoyed great popularity in Europe, America, and Australia during the nineteenth century. In mosaic patchwork, paper templates are cut to the finished size, then covered with a slightly larger piece of fabric, the edges of which are

The 1718 coverlet.

turned over the paper and basted into place. The edges of the fabric-covered papers are whipstitched together, and then the basting and templates are usually removed.

Mosaic patchwork was generally practiced by upper-class women. Both paper and fabric were expensive until technological developments increased availability and lowered the cost of both in the second half of the nineteenth century. By the end of the century, middle- and lower-class women were also making quilts. Although mosaic patchwork had fallen out of favor in this country by then, some quiltmakers adopted a different patchwork technique using paper. This method of "string" patchwork typically involved cutting relatively large shapes from newspaper or magazine pages. The shapes were then covered with a series of parallel strips of fabric, overlapping the fabrics and sewing through the paper, either by hand or by machine. The fabric is trimmed evenly with the edges of the paper and the fabric-covered papers are sewn together conventionally, rather than being whipstitched together.

Although string patchwork appears to have been a logical innovation derived from an increased availability of paper and fabric, an early New England quilt suggests that the use of paper in conventional patchwork is not so new after all. The collection of the Society for the Preservation of New England Antiquities in Boston includes an unquilted coverlet in which right-triangles of silk have been backed with newspaper then sewn together in a conventional manner. The paper templates appear to have provided stability for the thin, slippery silk. The piece may well have been considered complete as it is, or it may have been left unfinished for some reason. The newspapers date from the eighteenth century, and although the dates for the silk fabrics have not been confirmed, all indications suggest that this is indeed a very early example of American patchwork.

This elegant silk patchwork was clearly the work of someone who had access to expensive materials and a desire to make the corners of the slippery silk behave. Surviving examples of string patchwork from a century later have generally been interpreted as the work of less fortunate women who used random fabrics because it was all they had and lacked the initiative or skill to use regular pieced patterns. Throughout the twentieth century, string patchwork has served as a humble utility technique, although it offers intriguing design possibilities.

Anita Grossman Solomon and I each have collections of examples of twentieth century string patchwork tops and remnants. These may look rough and random, but a closer

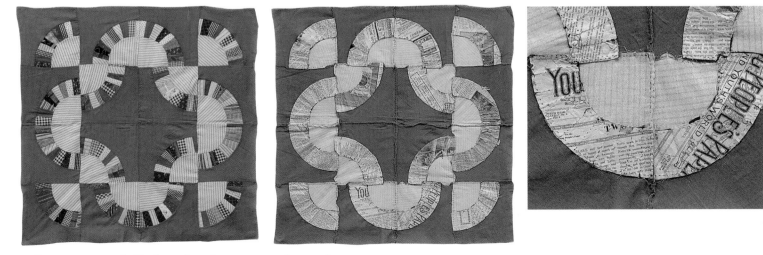

Baby Bunting *quilt block, early 20ᵗʰ century, 26½" x 26½".*

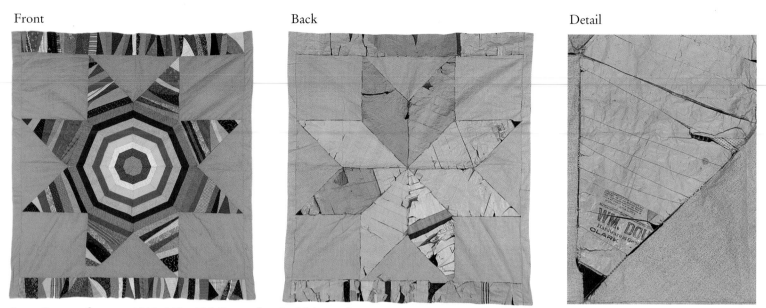

Front   Back   Detail

Lone Star *quilt top*, c. 1910. 84" x 78", Pennsylvania. Maker unknown.

look sometimes reveals the maker's intention. Anita owns an unquilted string-pieced Lone Star top thought to have been made in Pennsylvania around 1910.

The outer points of the star and the two borders are made up of irregular, non-parallel strips of many different printed fabrics, suggesting a lack of concern about precision and regularity. However, the inner points of the large diamonds are pieced of very evenly placed strips of bright solid color fabrics, forming a precise, regular pattern of concentric octagons radiating outward from the center. Although we don't know anything about the maker or her circumstances, the quilt top suggests that she enjoyed "playing" with her fabric, setting up a contrast between her star's regular center and irregular extremities.

In retrospect, it seems that our ancestors were neither self-conscious purists nor unsophisticated primitives. They approached quiltmaking much as we do today. They were aware of the work of previous generations but also willing to experiment with new techniques and materials. As with any tradition, people are willing to adopt innovations that seem to work, that offer some advantage, or provide a perceived benefit.

Anita Grossman Solomon offers a new approach to paper piecing in this book. Her technique may be enjoyed either as a re-introduction of a technique practiced by our ancestors or as the latest variation on the hottest innovation of recent years. So prepare yourself to enjoy experimenting with a new technique using paper—just like our ancestors did!

Pair of Lozenges pieced on "Funny Pages." 1929, 5 1/4" x 11".

Laurel Horton is a folklorist and internationally known quilt researcher. Her research includes regional variations on quiltmaking traditions, historical South Carolina quilts, and contemporary quilts by dance groups. She has been making string quilts since 1979 and teaches this technique regularly.

INTRODUCTION

In the fall of 1990, I happened to be walking past a shop with French decorating fabrics located on Bleecker Street in New York City. There was a sign in the window indicating that it was their last day of business. I had never been in the store before, but when I saw all the shoppers inside, I couldn't resist the temptation to take a look for myself. The next thing I remember is fingering the scraps and yardage I'd bought as I rode the bus home. I was not a quilter at that time.

For fun, I thought I'd piece the scraps into a quilt and then toss the leftover pieces. Fate had other intentions for me.

Quilter's Passion, a New York City quilt shop now closed, was also a milestone in my quilting evolution. More fabric came into my life. Small New York City apartment. Big trouble.

I came across the Pineapple block foundation papers at Quilter's Passion. I was not familiar with the pattern and didn't know what a finished block would look like. I completed four strangely-colored blocks and I've been hooked on paper piecing ever since. I began to make my own foundation patterns, combining my interest in quilting with my interest in the computer. This proved to be an inspired pairing. One thing led to another until twelve years later I found myself writing this book.

I spend days and nights thinking about quilting, especially as I drift off to sleep. This is when I think of blocks, settings and quilting designs. Often I get so stirred up with ideas that I can't sleep, and at that point, I make myself concentrate on an image of a sewing machine making one perfect stitch after another in slow motion. The repetitive perpetual motion sends me to dreamland. Why count sheep when I can count stitches?

While I was lying in bed one night thinking about the Zegart block (see page 97), I realized that I had no pattern for it. As I thought about how to break up the block for paper piecing, suddenly its "X" frame and diagonal lines stood out as if in neon relief. Thus was born the idea for *Make It Simpler Paper Piecing*.

When I explain the concept of not cutting up the foundations to paper piecers their reaction is invariably, "Why didn't I think of that?" A moment later, they ask, "How did YOU think of it?" They want to try it immediately. I love to see them grin with satisfaction as their blocks come together almost effortlessly.

The quilt designs, foundation patterns, and templates for this book originated with EQ5, a computer software program from The Electric Quilt Company. The patterns with a "Brackman number" can be found in *BlockBase*, an electronic version of *Barbara Brackman's Encyclopedia of Pieced Quilt Patterns*.

Please take advantage of the extensive advice and techniques outlined in the beginning of the book. My advice to sew one thread over, is particularly effective in achieving the most perfect centers that I've ever made. Piecing quilt blocks is a labor of love for me and I hope that you will share my enthusiasm for this technique.

THE MAKE IT SIMPLER
Techniques
for Paper Piecing

EXPERIENCED PAPER PIECERS

Before you make a block read this advice and adjust your routine with these important steps.

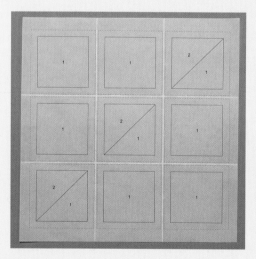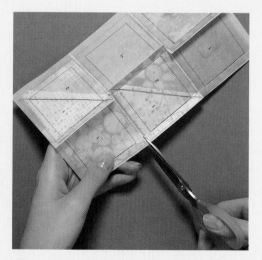

1. Do not cut the foundation into subunits. Crease the foundation along the 4 dotted lines that separate the 9 subunits.

2. Work from a mock-up. Cut the fabric exactly to the template sizes—no oversized pieces. Make sure there is no fabric in the gutter.

3. Like hand piecers, never sew across the interior seam allowances. Clip foundations at previously sewn intersections before attempting to re-fold and sew perpendicular seams.

Nine-patch Variation 1706

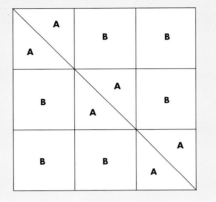

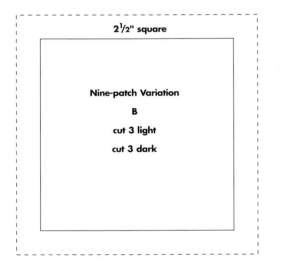

2½" square

Nine-patch Variation

B

cut 3 light

cut 3 dark

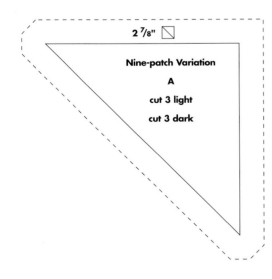

2⅞" ◻

Nine-patch Variation

A

cut 3 light

cut 3 dark

HELPFUL HINTS

Replacing the two triangles in the center square with a simple 2½" square of red fabric creates the "Split Nine-patch" block, native to New Jersey. Like the traditional Log Cabin, the Nine-patch Variation and the Split Nine-patch can be arranged in Barn Raising and Streak of Lightning settings. The Straight Furrows setting is more versatile since it can be made with an odd number of blocks.

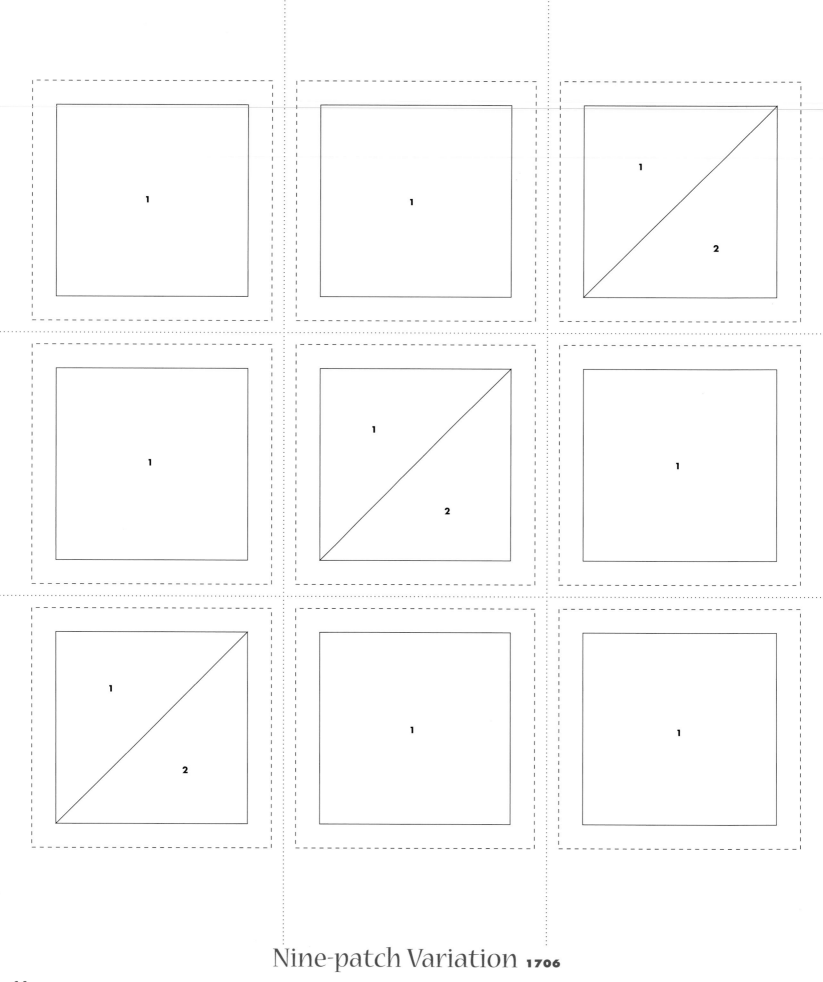

Nine-patch Variation 1706

Nine-patch Variations being assembled by my nephews Seth—5, Adam—8, and Josh—10.

Getting Started

The Nine-patch Variation is a traditional block dating from the nineteenth century. It is simple to make and demonstrates the Make It Simple Paper Piecing techniques used to construct the other blocks in this book.

If you are new to paper piecing, try the Nine-patch Variation. If you've had experience paper piecing, try a block that you've made in the past to compare construction techniques. The more challenging blocks have more seams converging in the center, such as the Hunter's Star, the Pinwheel, and the Stauber Star.

Preparation

1. Photocopy a foundation pattern from the book onto translucent paper. To evaluate the accuracy of the copy machine, superimpose the copy on top of the original. If the lines match up perfectly, make additional photocopies of the pattern onto translucent paper. You will need at least 1 for the mock-up and 1 for sewing. Don't copy a photocopy of a foundation; always use the original from the book to keep copier distortion to a minimum. Copy the templates onto ordinary paper.

❖ TIP

May I photocopy the foundation patterns onto white copy paper instead of onto translucent paper? Well, you wouldn't be making it simpler. It is more difficult to crease and fold copy paper and you can't see through it very well. Nothing beats translucent paper for ease. I would also avoid using different brands of foundation paper during a project, because they may not yield identical results. To avoid confusion prepare, copy, and label separate templates for A (regular) and AR (reversed)

❖ TIP

Do I have to worry about "mirror imaging" when I photocopy? No. The foundations in the book are already mirrored for you.

2. Trim away excess foundation paper, leaving about $3/4"$ around the block. This makes sewing at the machine more manageable.

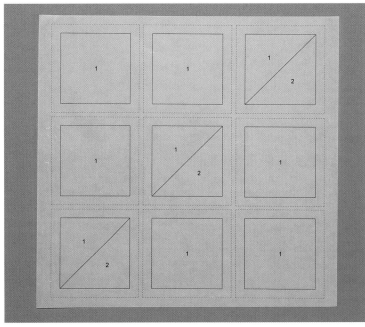

Trim the foundation.

3. Fold and crease the foundation. Always crease the foundation paper before sewing. The dotted lines on the pattern indicate the fold lines. First fold the unprinted sides of the foundation together. The seam and fold lines are easier to see this way. Then fold the same line, placing printed sides together and crease sharply. Repeat for all fold lines. The printed lines are more visible on a light table or white surface. I fold my foundation against the TV screen. While the TV is on, static electricity holds the foundation in place—almost like a third hand.

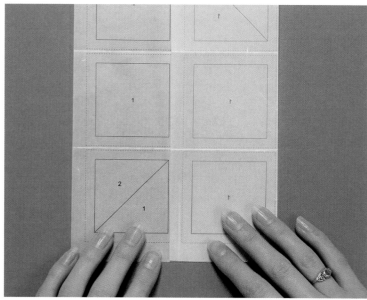

Fold and crease on vertical fold lines.

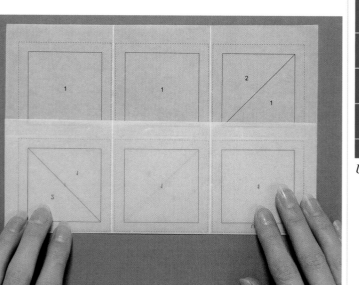

Fold and crease on horizontal fold lines.

4. Choose and cut the fabrics. For each block, select 6 light and 6 dark fabrics. Cut 3 light and 3 dark 2½" squares. Also cut 3 light and 3 dark 2⅞" squares, then cut these diagonally in half. Use the triangle template to trim off the base points so they won't extend into the gutter. You will have 6 triangles leftover.

▨ TIP

How do you make and use the templates?
Photocopy the templates on regular copy paper and cut them out. If a template gets misplaced, just make another copy of it. First, cut the fabric using the dimensions on the template. Then, place the template flush along the edge of the fabric. Trim off the excess fabric around the template with your rotary cutter, use a ruler to protect your fingers when necessary. You could also hold the template and fabric in one hand while trimming off the excess with a pair of scissors.

Use the template to cut off excess fabric.

Cut fabric for only one block right now. This will give you the opportunity to alter your fabric choices or to modify your cutting plan.

I use a 2½" acrylic square to cut many squares at one time from scraps. For the triangles, I cut (or sometimes tear) a strip from the yardage almost ½" wider than necessary since I don't want to wrestle with a large piece of fabric. If I have a ½ yard of fabric, I tear it along the length so that I have a piece measuring about 18" x 3½". I prefer strips from the length (parallel to the selvage) because I find them more stable to work with than strips cut along the width. I fold the strip to a length that I can comfortably cut 2⅞" squares from. I usually cut through 5 layers of fabric at once and then cut on the diagonal to yield 10 triangles.

> ### 🔲 TIP
>
> **Since I can easily gauge the fabric to cut for the template shapes, must I pay attention to the rotary cutting information?** Yes, it's a matter of ensuring good grain line placement in the block especially when it comes to triangles. Depending on their placement in the block, different cuts of triangles are required. Half-square triangles are made from squares cut once on the diagonal to yield a pair of triangles. Each will have only 1 side on the bias. Quarter-square triangles are made from cutting a square of fabric twice, on each diagonal. This yields 4 triangles, each with 2 bias sides.

Half-square Triangle   Quarter-square Triangle

5. Make a fabric mock-up by placing the cut squares and triangles on the unprinted side of an unfolded foundation. The Nine-patch Variation visually divides the block into 2 large triangles, 1 of which reads darker (or lighter) than the other.

> ### 🔲 TIP
>
> **What is a mock-up?** A mock-up is a preview of the completed block. The entire block is laid out in position prior to sewing. It's an opportunity to view the relationship of 1 fabric to another to check color harmonies, interactions between fabrics, and to correct placement.

Mock-up of block.

> ### 🔲 TIP
>
> **I have paper pieced before and I know where every fabric is to go. I want to skip making a mock-up. Is that ok?** Skipping the mock-up was often my downfall causing me a lot of wasted effort on blocks that didn't work.

Sew

Which side of the foundation do you sew on? You will always be sewing on the printed side of the foundation. It will be the back of the block when you have finished. The unprinted side is the side that the fabric is glued to. You can see through the translucent foundation paper, but the numbers or words will appear backwards.

1. Set up the sewing machine with a #90 needle. Set the stitch length to approximately 15–20 stitches per inch. Use a neutral color thread such as medium gray, both on the top and in the bobbin.

2. Pick up a light triangle from the mock-up. Position it, right side up, on the unprinted side of another foundation in the corresponding location. Lightly glue the tips of the triangles down. Glue the remaining 2 light triangles into place. You can also use pins if you prefer.

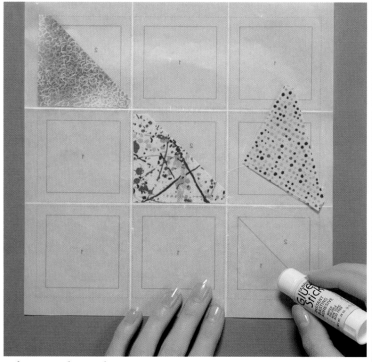

Glue triangles in place.

🔳 TIP

Should I use any special gluestick? It must be washable, not permanent. I prefer Collins Fabric Glue Stick. Whatever brand you use, it should go on smoothly. If it leaves clumps of glue, use a fresh gluestick.

Put glue on the two seam allowances at the same time. Then place triangles right sides together.

🔳 TIP

Why do you glue rather than pin? It's simpler! Pins make a small bump in the paper foundation and they just get in the way.

3. Place the dark triangles, right sides down, on the top of their corresponding light triangles. The fabric must never extend over any fold line although it's okay if it doesn't completely cover the seam allowance. Glue the dark triangles to the light triangles within the ¼" seam allowance on the diagonal, or re-pin to secure both the light and dark triangles to the foundation.

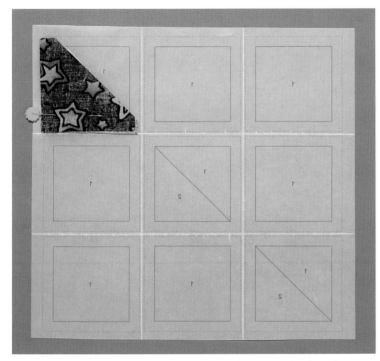

You can use pins or gluestick to secure the fabrics to the foundation.

✦ TIP

Can I sew now? Yes, but before you sew, check to be sure the fabric didn't shift when you turned the foundation over.

Here's what happened when I neglected to glue a piece of fabric to the foundation. It slipped out of place when I sewed the next triangle onto it.

4. Turn the foundation paper over and sew a continuous diagonal line through the paper betweeen #1 and #2 to join the triangles. In this instance, you can sew through the seam allowances. Begin and end the stitching beyond the seam allowances at the edge of the block.

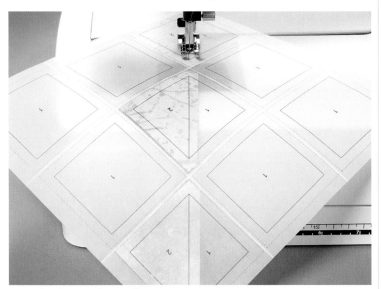

Sew the diagonal seam line.

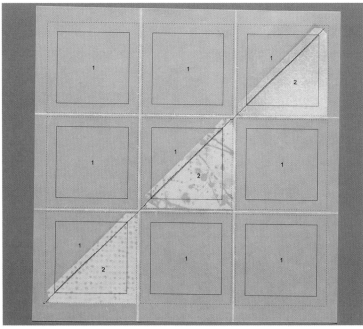

Sewn block.

5. Press the sewn triangles open with an iron (no steam). If your fabric was starched before you began, you can simply finger-press the triangles open.

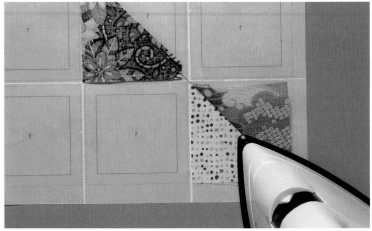

Press the triangle units open.

6. Lightly glue the triangle **corners** to the paper.

Glue the corners down.

7. Move the 6 fabric squares from the mock-up and lightly glue them in place on the foundation.

Move the squares over from the mock-up and glue them down.

Joining the Subunits

The 9 subunits are complete. Check to make sure there is no excess fabric lying in the gutter covering a fold line. If there is, it is essential that you trim the excess fabric back within the seam allowance. No pins from now on!

The subunits are complete.

1. With the fabric side of the foundation face up, fold 1 of the 4 creased lines so that the fabric remains in place and is enclosed in the paper and the printed sewing lines are facing you.

Fold the foundation over, enclosing the fabric.

2. Begin sewing at the top of the block, at least $1/8$" beyond the outside seam allowance. It's not necessary to backstitch. Sew towards the opposite side of the block, sewing through the first outside seam allowance. Do not sew across any interior seam allowances.

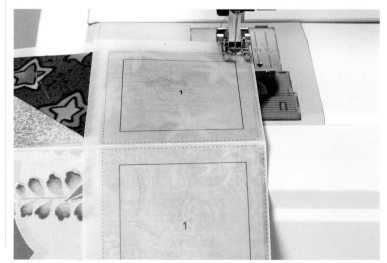

Sew the first seam.

3. Continue to sew, raising the needle and passing over each of the two interior seam allowances. Stop at the end of a seam, raise the needle and presser foot, and without clipping the thread, move across the seam allowance. Sew through the final seam allowance at the edge of the block, and continue sewing for at least 1/8" beyond the outside seam allowance line. Do not sew across any interior seam allowances.

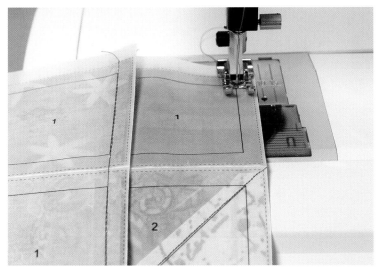

The first seam has been sewn. The needle passed over, not through, the seam allowance. Sew the second seam.

4. Now that you have sewn both parallel seams, make a perpendicular clip at least 3/8" into each of the 4 intersections. Nothing bad will happen. An intersection occurs when one fold line crosses another fold line.

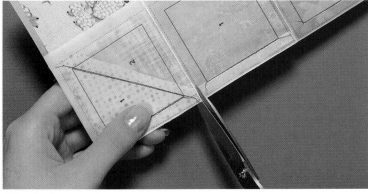

Clip the intersections.

5. Press the seams in alternating directions. Use a pressing cloth on top of the printed side of the foundation if the iron melts the printing ink.

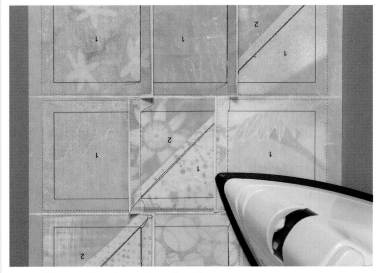

Press the seams in alternating directions.

6. Fold one of the unsewn sides, enclosing the fabric again. It will fold over easily because you snipped the intersection. Sew this seam without sewing any of the flaps down. Pause while sewing to push the flaps away from the needle. Backstitch before and after the flap, on the same line, if you wish.

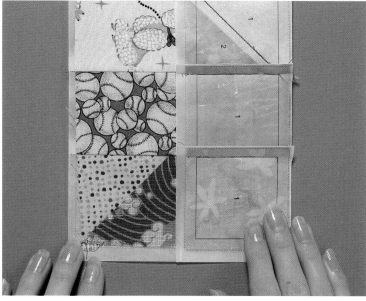

Fold the foundation over, enclosing the fabric.

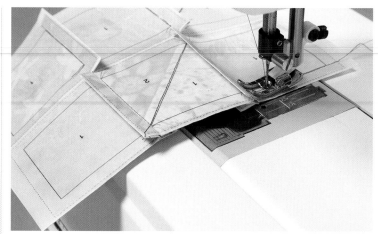

Sew the remaining seams, passing over each of the interior seam allowances.

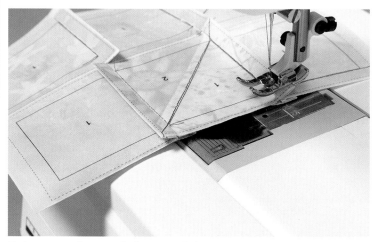

Raise presser foot, push flap out of the way.

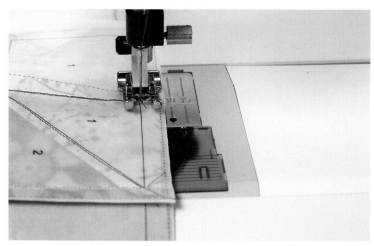

Continue stitching.

Press the block open.

7. True up the blocks to 6½" square. During the construction of the block, the paper may have decreased in size. Center a 6½" acrylic square on the back side of the block (fabric side is down) and use this as a guide to trim the block. Never rely on the printed edge of the foundation as a trimming guide. You may find some seam allowances weren't completely covered by fabric.

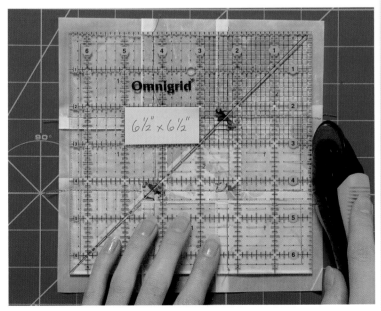

Trim the finished block.

Finished block.

8. Do not remove the foundation paper until after the entire quilt top has been sewn together. You may remove the folded paper enclosing the seams to help press the seams open or to the side.

9. After you have completed all the blocks for your project, join the blocks by sewing a ¼" seam parallel to the edge of the paper. Line the blocks up along the edges of the paper foundations. The fabric may not come out to the edge of the block, so leaving the paper in place gives you an accurate guide for sewing. As you stitch the blocks together, you may remove the paper when you reach an area where you might be sewing more that 2 layers of paper together.

Ask Anita

1. **What is the most important step to remember?**
First you need to fold and crease the foundation. If you forget this step, unthread the needle and stitch through the fold line to needle punch the foundation after-the-fact.

2. **What makes one block easier to make than another?** The easier blocks have one to two pieces per subunit and fewer seams and intersections.

3. **What makes a block suitable for Make It Simpler Paper Piecing?** The block needs to have a seam line running continuously through it from one side to the other, either diagonally, horizontally, or vertically.

4. **I'm only using two different fabrics in my block. Do I have to make a mock-up?** Yes, it's a big help. You also might want to make a notation on your foundation as to where each color is placed. Use a permanent pen, since pencil can smudge and ballpoint ink may bleed when ironed.

5. **What is a subunit?** A subunit is a section of the whole block. A block is divided into subunits for construction. For example the Nine-patch Variation has 9 subunits, while Jan's Star, the block on the cover, has 4 subunits. After all of the subunits have been assembled, they are joined to make the block. In conventional paper piecing, the subunits are cut apart, pieced, trimmed and then carefully joined together again. But with my technique, the subunits are never cut apart. With a few folds—no pinning necessary—the subunits come together perfectly.

6. **Can I set up more than 1 unit to save time?** Yes. Set up all the #1 and #2 pieces on the block at the same time. You can even set up more than 1 block in this manner at a time.

7. **What determines piecing order?** Piecing order is like mopping the kitchen floor. You don't want to end up in the middle of the floor. I have numbered all the blocks with a piecing sequence, but there is often more than one possible way to piece a subunit. I prefer to begin piecing at the perimeter to first cover the edge of the block with fabric, then piece towards the center. If I have an especially awkward shape to cover, I will start there if possible. The Palm and the Stauber Star blocks are best pieced clockwise or counterclockwise so their opposing seams fit together

8. **How can I avoid shadowing?** When a dark and light fabric are to be sewn together, place the dark fabric on top of the lighter one and then stitch them together. For example, when 2 triangles are sewn together to form a subunit in the Nine-patch Variation block, start by positioning the light fabric, face up, first. Then place the dark fabric, face down, on top of it. After sewing, trim back the dark fabric in the seam allowance and brush away any dark threads if they are visible.

9. **Is it necessary to cover the seam allowances completely with fabric?** No, as long as you end up with at least $1/8$" of fabric extending beyond the seam. When the block is trued up, it will be $6^{1}/_2$" x $6^{1}/_2$" square. You will sew blocks together using the edge of the paper as your guide, not the fabric.

10. **Is there anything I can do to make sure I fill the seam allowance along the outside edge?** Yes, begin piecing the subunit with the fabric that falls along the outside edge, when practical.

11. **Is there an order to joining the subunits to complete the block?** Sew your choice of parallel seams first, whether they are horizontal or vertical. Clip the intersections and then sew the perpendicular seams.

12. **What about your "one thread over" trick?** When sewing a seam, don't sew right on the line because the thread of the stitching takes up space. Your block ends up slightly smaller than it should. You can lose the tip points. Instead, sew one thread-width over the line into the seam allowance either when sewing the long seams to join subunits or when sewing blocks into a quilt top. When piecing some subunits (say sewing piece #2 to piece #1)

there is no seam allowance for you to sew one thread over into. Instead sew one thread over into the area that is to be covered by fabric (the area piece #2 is to occupy, and so forth)

13. Why must I sew only the seam lines and not sew through the seam allowances when I get to an intersection? You'll have three advantages: Less bulk at the intersection, the flexibility to press the seam allowances to either side, and an easier time removing the paper when you've finished.

14. Why should I true up my block with a 6½" acrylic square? Because the foundation may have decreased in size during construction and the printed lines may no longer be accurate guidelines.

15. Will my rotary cutter become dull from cutting the translucent paper? Yes. I work with two medium-size rotary cutters, one for paper and one for fabric.

16. Do I need to stitch the edge of my block once the sewing is complete? No. If the edge fabric is on the bias or is not lying flat, lightly glue it in place. Extra stitching around the edges makes it harder to remove the paper.

17. What if I make a mistake and need to rip out a seam? On the paper side, cover the sewn seam with a piece of removable Scotch Magic Tape (blue plaid box). Remove the errant stitches, then remove the tape and re-sew the seam with a longer stitch length. Never iron a block that has tape on it.

18. Why should I use a pressing sheet? Sometimes the toner in the photocopy machine will melt on contact with the iron during pressing and will transfer onto the block. Grrrr. A pressing cloth between your iron and the block will prevent this from happening.

Ruined block with toner marks.

19. Do you prewash your fabric? I wash, dry, starch, and iron all of my fabric. I like the way it handles after it's been primed.

LEGEND

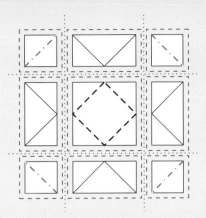

☐ First cut a square the size indicated on the template pattern, then cut in half once on the diagonal to yield half-square triangles

☒ First cut a square the size indicated on the template pattern, then cut it diagonally twice to yield quarter-square triangles.

Fold line ··

Outside line - - - - - - - - - - - -

Design line for alternate block in multiple block pattern. ·-·-·-·-·-·-·

Design line for alternate block in multiple block pattern. - - - - - - - - -

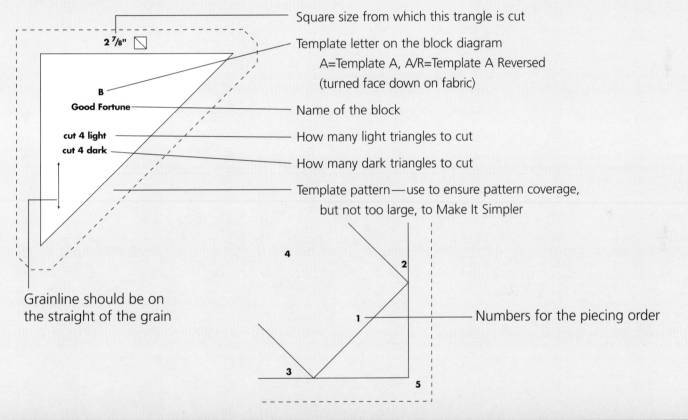

Square size from which this trangle is cut

2 7/8" ☐

Template letter on the block diagram
A=Template A, A/R=Template A Reversed
(turned face down on fabric)

B

Good Fortune ────────── Name of the block

cut 4 light ────────── How many light triangles to cut

cut 4 dark ────────── How many dark triangles to cut

────────── Template pattern—use to ensure pattern coverage, but not too large, to Make It Simpler

Grainline should be on the straight of the grain

4   2

1 ──────── Numbers for the piecing order

3   5

SUPPLY LIST

Good Fortune 1184

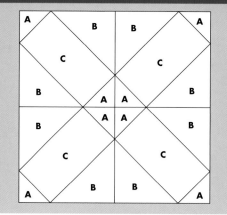

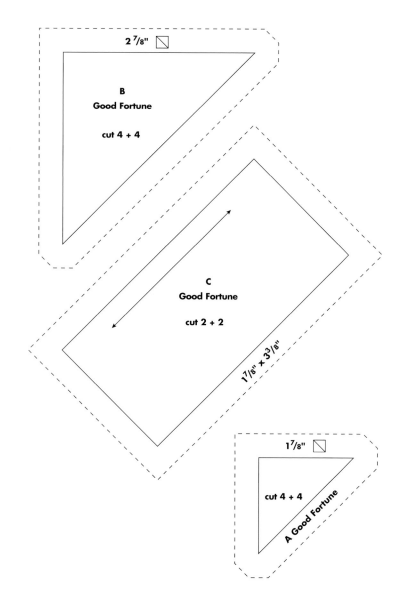

2 7/8"

B
Good Fortune

cut 4 + 4

C
Good Fortune

cut 2 + 2

1 7/8" × 3 3/8"

1 7/8"

cut 4 + 4

A Good Fortune

HELPFUL HINTS

The lines yield a strikingly dynamic design when you use the setting shown here. Trim the darker fabric slightly under the lighter fabric to avoid shadowing.

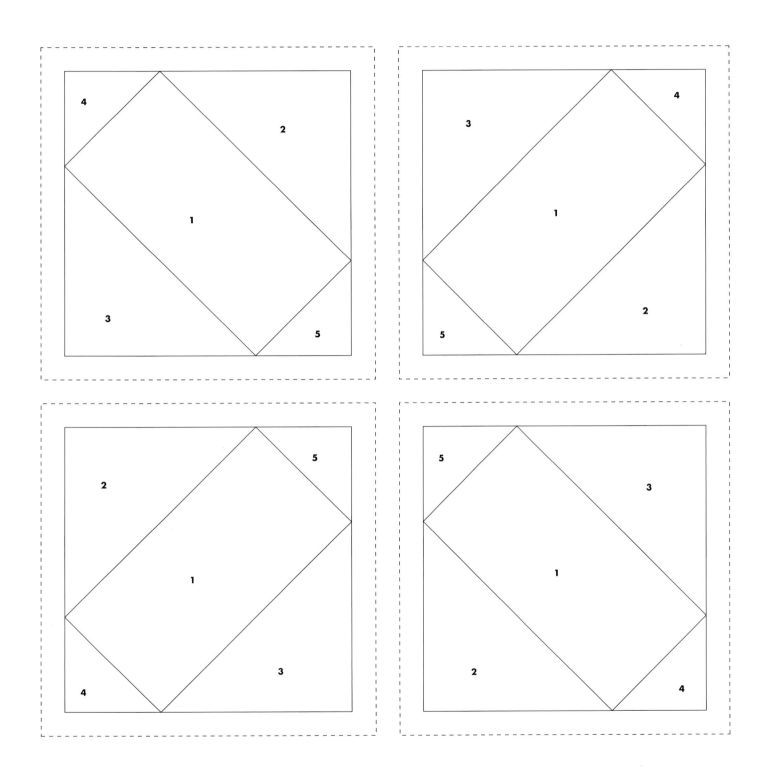

Good Fortune 1184

Crossed Canoes 1251

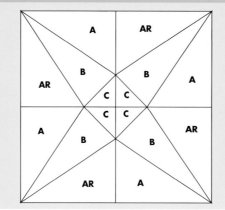

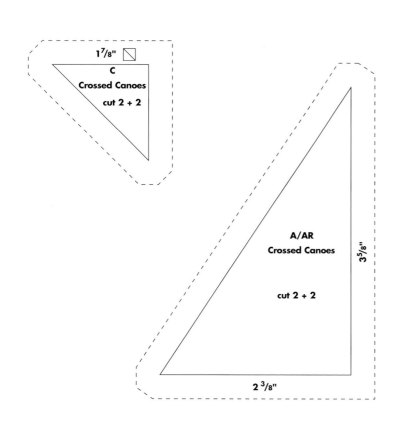

1⁷/₈"

C
Crossed Canoes

cut 2 + 2

A/AR
Crossed Canoes

cut 2 + 2

3⁵/₈"

2³/₈"

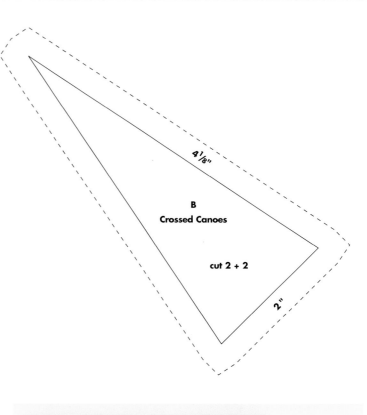

4¹/₈"

B
Crossed Canoes

cut 2 + 2

2"

HELPFUL HINTS

To avoid bulk in the center, press the seams open. When sewing the two long sides of the canoe, don't sew exactly on the line, rather use the "one thread-over" trick. See page 27.

Crossed Canoes **1251**

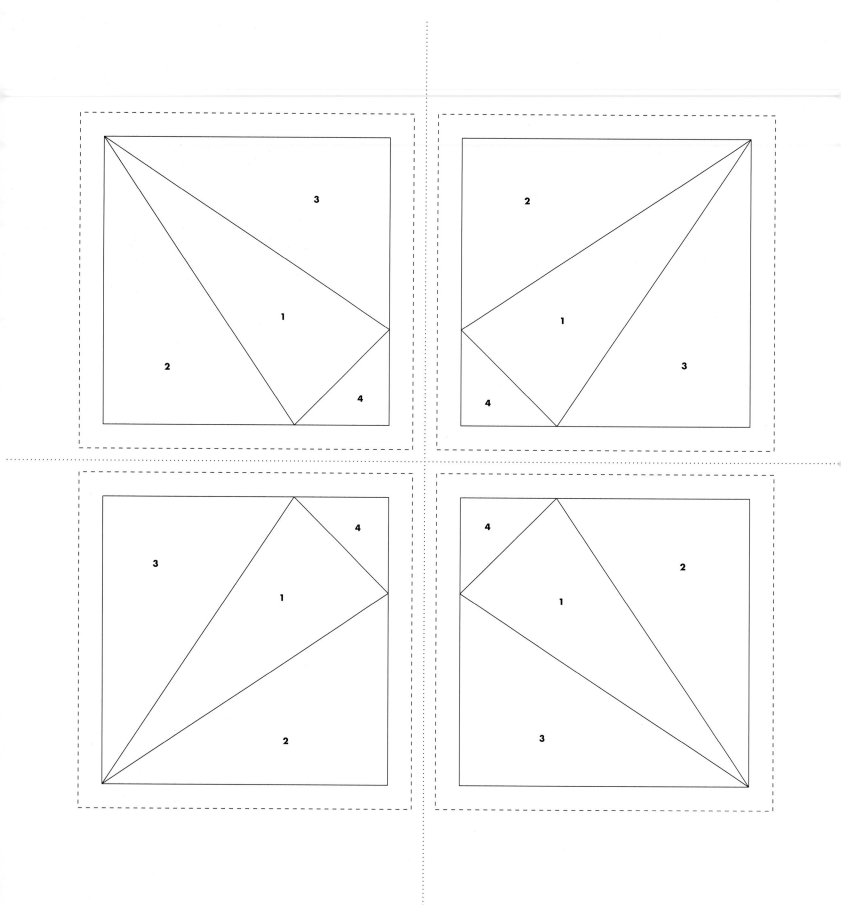

Crossed Canoes 1251

Make It Simpler Visits California 1116 (modified)

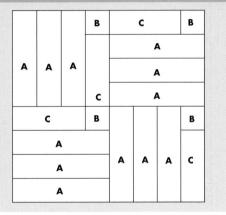

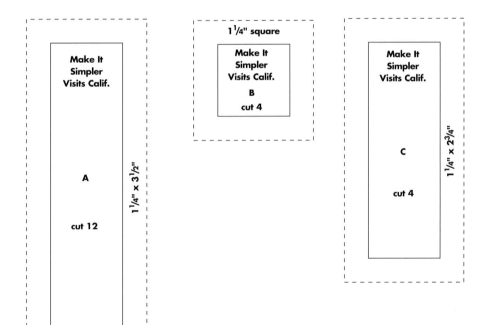

Make It
Simpler
Visits Calif.

A

cut 12

$1^1/4" \times 3^1/2"$

1/4" square

Make It
Simpler
Visits Calif.

B

cut 4

Make It
Simpler
Visits Calif.

C

cut 4

$1^1/4" \times 2^3/4"$

Make It Simpler Visits California 1116 (modified)

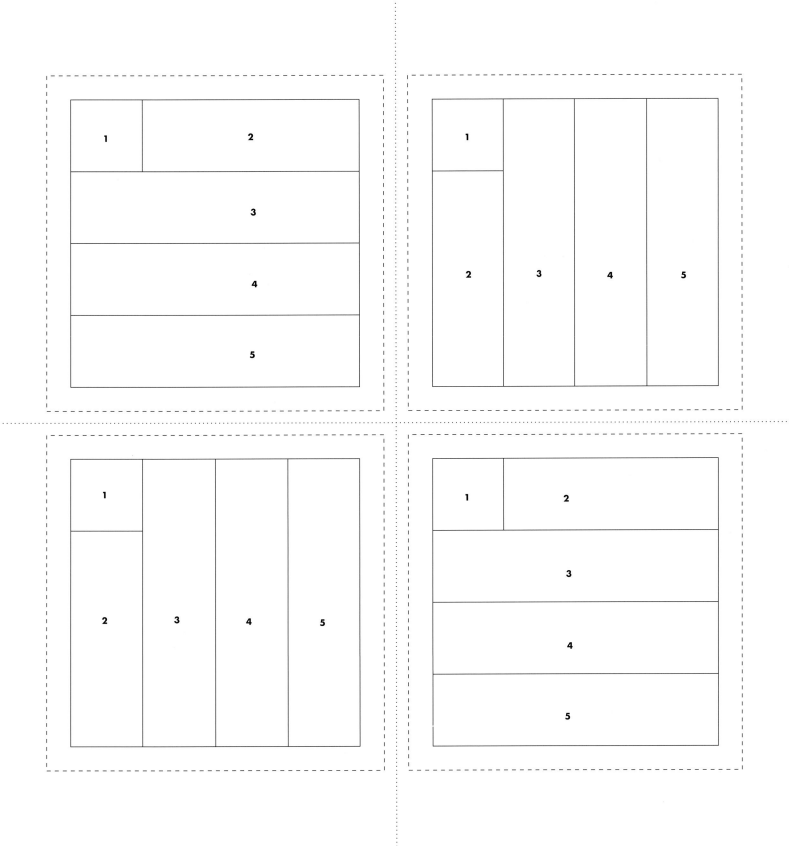

Make It Simpler Visits California 1116 (modified)

Dutchman's Puzzle 1339a

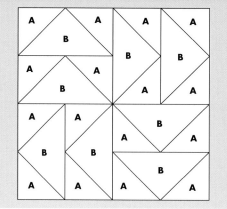

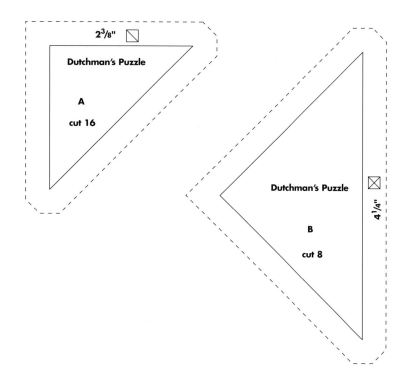

2³/₈"

Dutchman's Puzzle

A

cut 16

4¹/₄"

Dutchman's Puzzle

B

cut 8

Dutchman's Puzzle 1339a

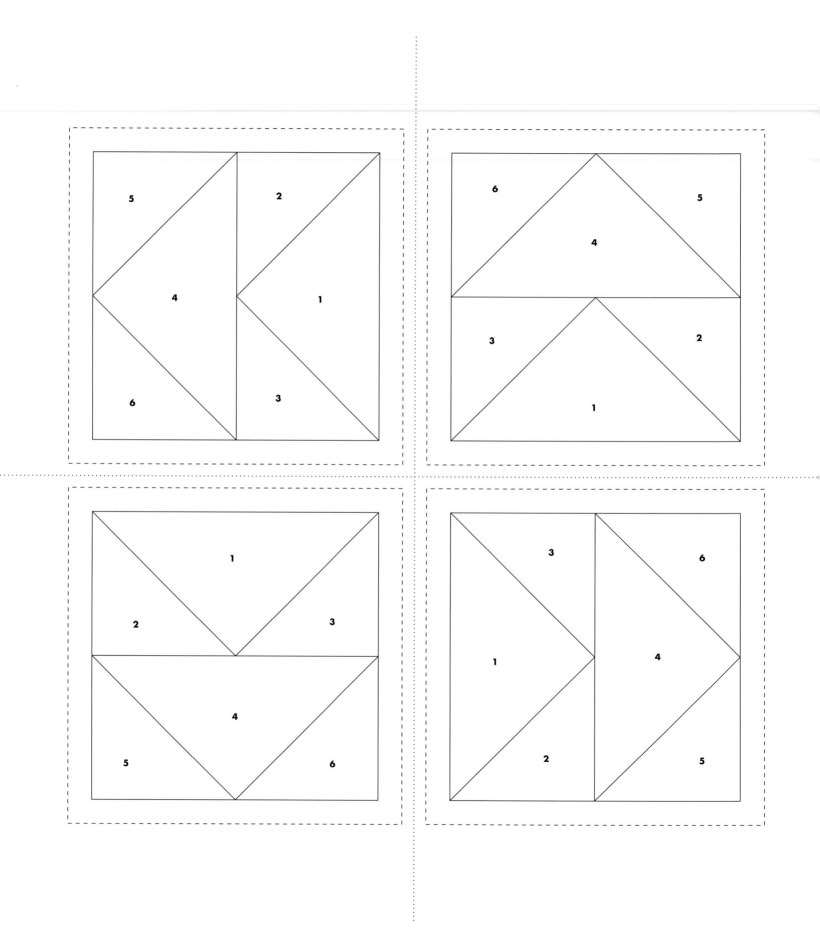

Dutchman's Puzzle 1339a

Storm at Sea 1071

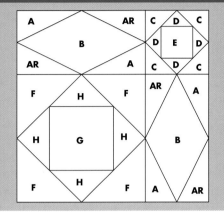

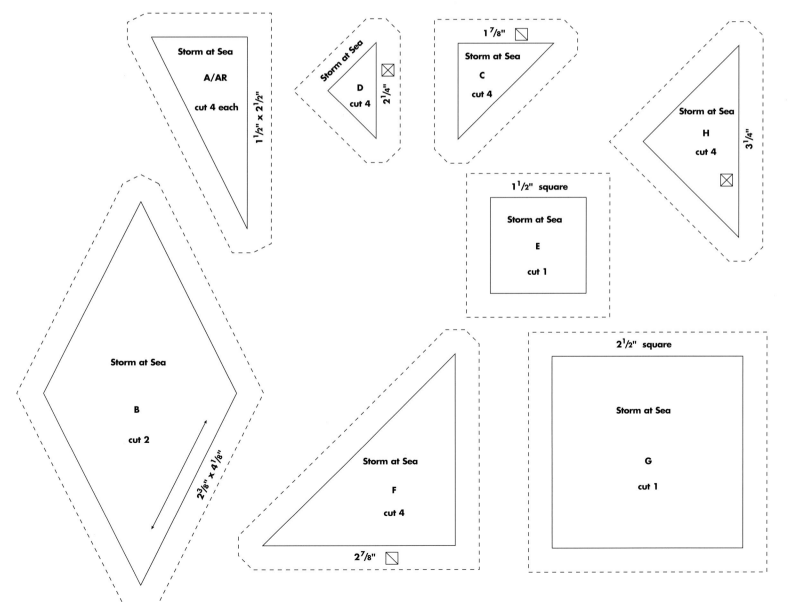

Storm at Sea
A/AR
cut 4 each
$1^{1}/2" \times 2^{1}/2"$

Storm at Sea
D
cut 4
$2^{1}/4"$

$1^{7}/8"$
Storm at Sea
C
cut 4

Storm at Sea
H
cut 4
$3^{1}/4"$

$1^{1}/2"$ square
Storm at Sea
E
cut 1

Storm at Sea
B
cut 2
$2^{3}/8" \times 4^{1}/8"$

Storm at Sea
F
cut 4
$2^{7}/8"$

$2^{1}/2"$ square
Storm at Sea
G
cut 1

Storm at Sea 1071

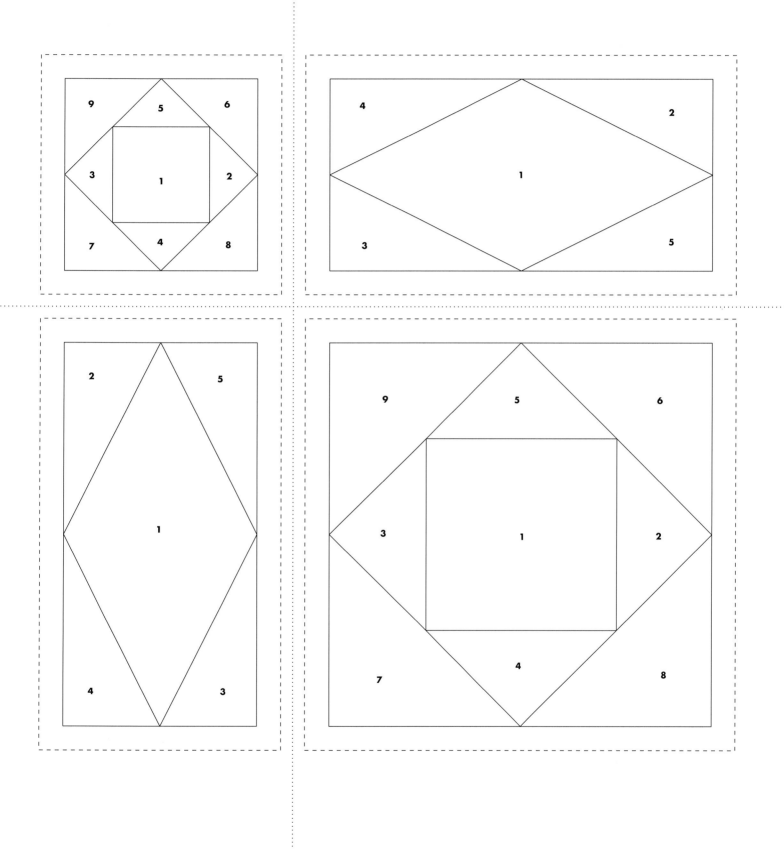

Storm at Sea 1071

Square Dance, Windmill Blades, Key West Beauty *2702, 2704, 2731*

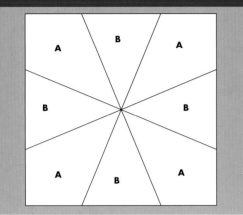
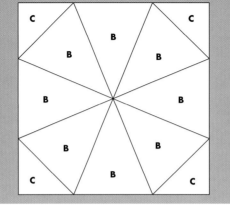
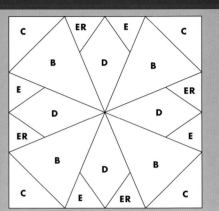

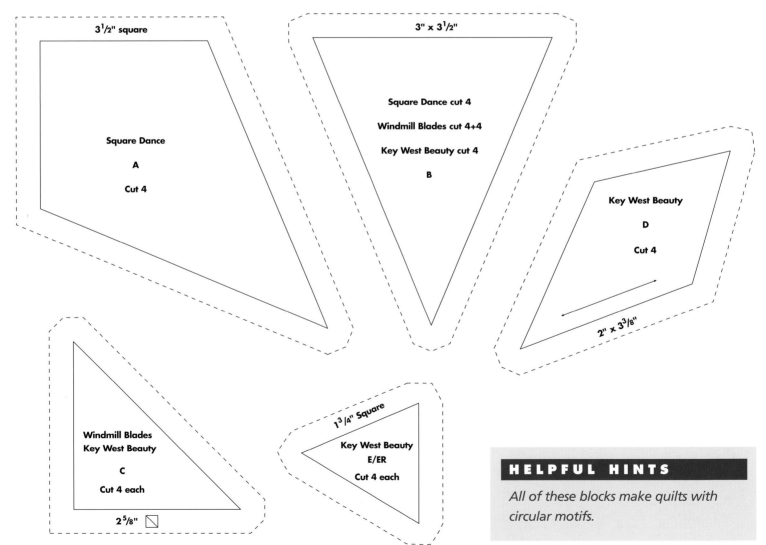

3½" square

Square Dance

A

Cut 4

3" x 3½"

Square Dance cut 4

Windmill Blades cut 4+4

Key West Beauty cut 4

B

Key West Beauty

D

Cut 4

2" x 3⅜"

Windmill Blades
Key West Beauty

C

Cut 4 each

2⅝"

1¾" Square

Key West Beauty
E/ER

Cut 4 each

HELPFUL HINTS

All of these blocks make quilts with circular motifs.

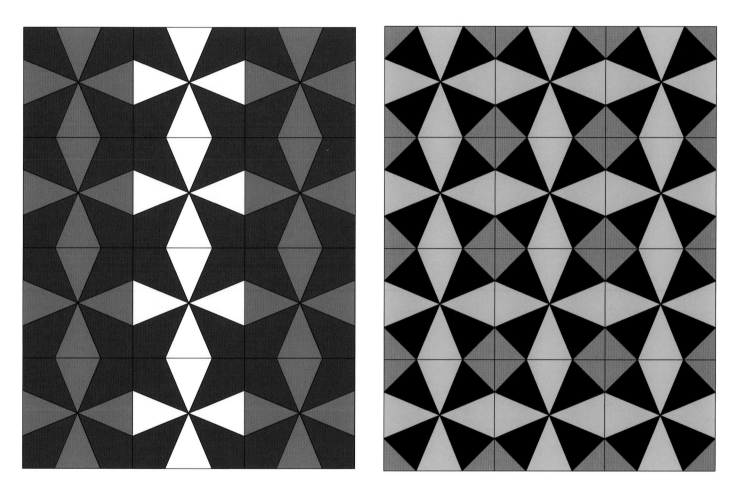

Square Dance; Windmill Blades *2702; 2704*

Key West Beauty 2731

Square Dance, Windmill Blades, Key West Beauty *2702, 2704, 2731*

Maple Leaf 1735

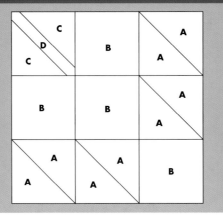

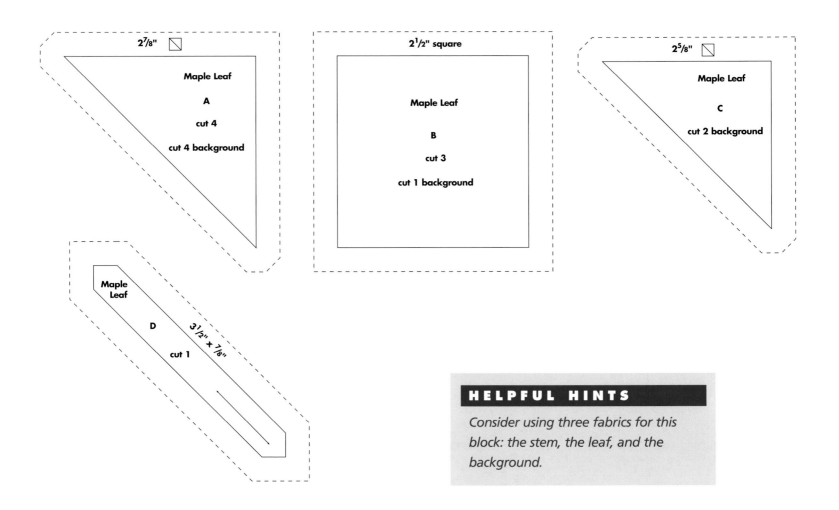

2⅞"

Maple Leaf

A

cut 4

cut 4 background

2½" square

Maple Leaf

B

cut 3

cut 1 background

2⅝"

Maple Leaf

C

cut 2 background

Maple Leaf

D

3½" × ⅞"

cut 1

HELPFUL HINTS

Consider using three fabrics for this block: the stem, the leaf, and the background.

Maple Leaf 1735

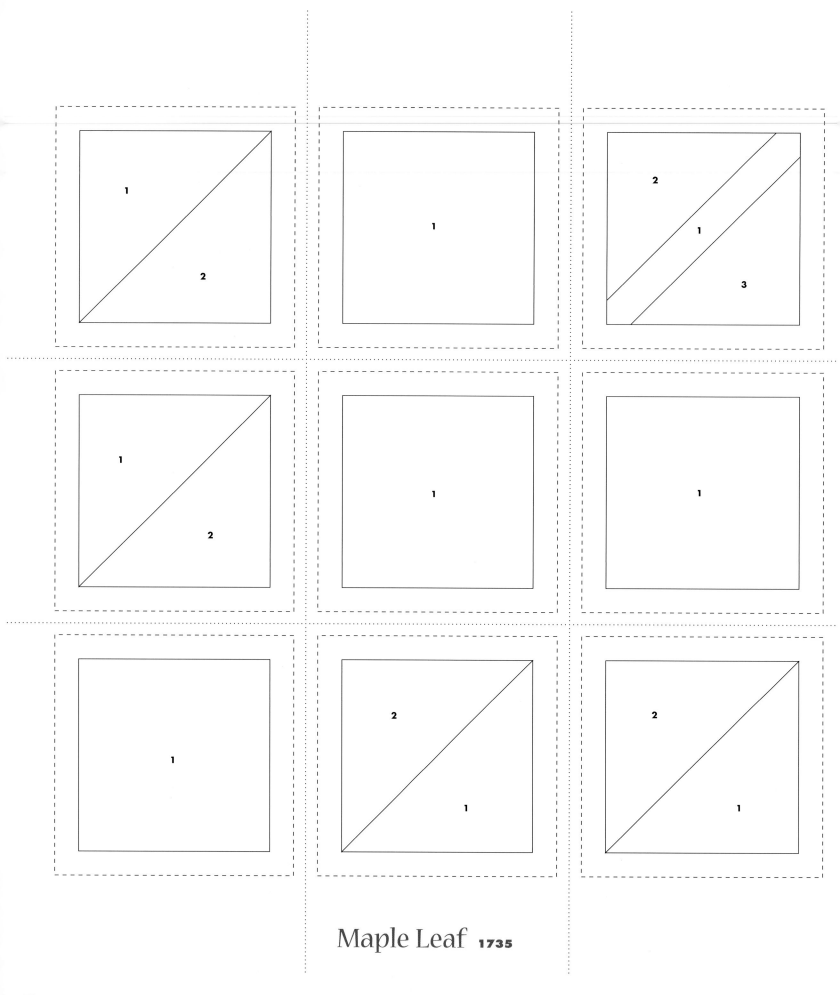

Maple Leaf 1735

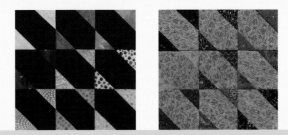

X-quisite 1001

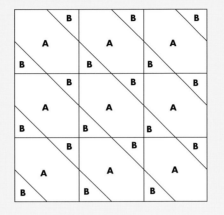

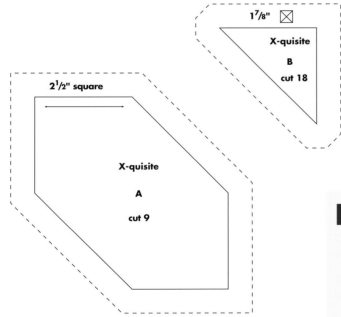

1⁷/₈" ⊠

X-quisite

B

cut 18

2¹/₂" square

X-quisite

A

cut 9

HELPFUL HINTS

To make the background lozenge shapes for each block (pattern A), cut nine 2¹/₂" squares of background fabric and stack as many as you can cut at one time. Place the template on top of the stack as a trimming guide. Place a ruler flush along the edge of the template and trim off the exposed triangle. Repeat to trim off the other triangle. You can assembly line piece this block when the background and triangles are cut using the templates. Glue all of the units, background pieces and triangles, into position and then sew all the seams in one operation.

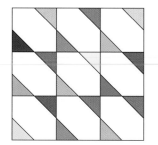

X-quisite **1001**

Hugs and Kisses, made by Marcella Peek, Belmont, CA.

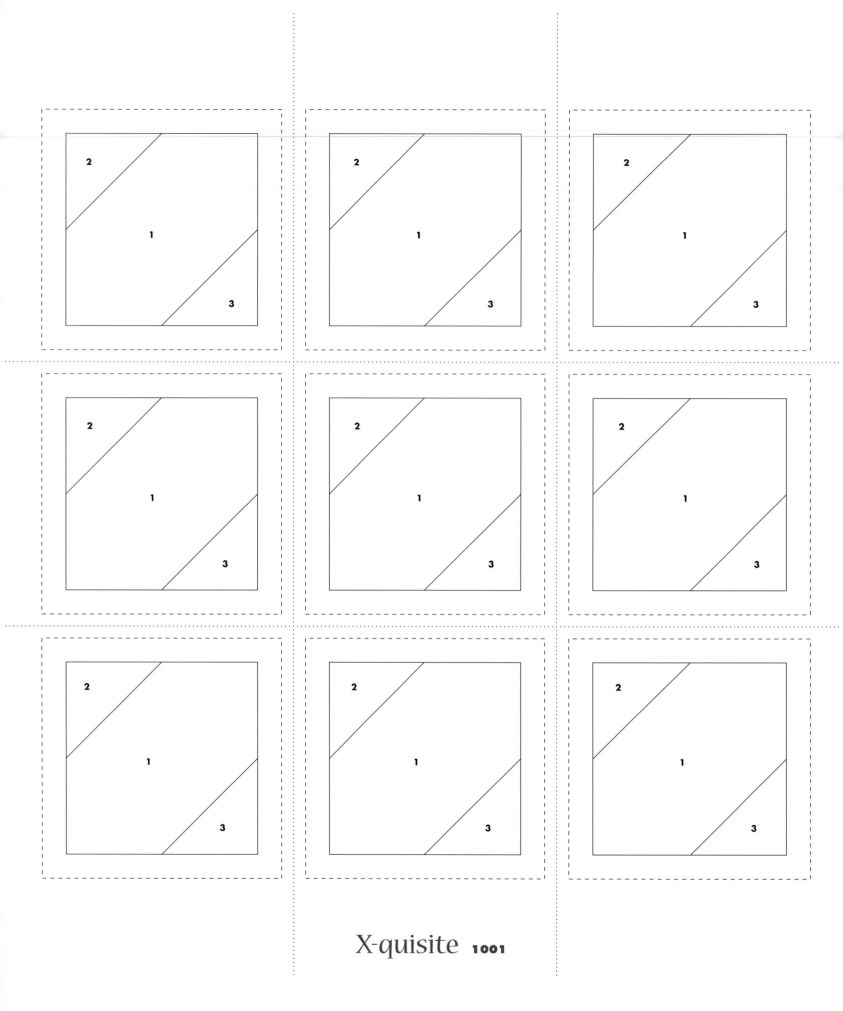

X-quisite 1001

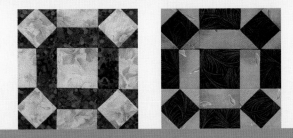

Rolling Stone 1727a

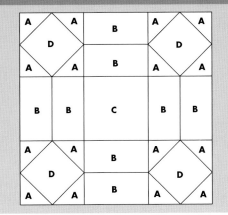

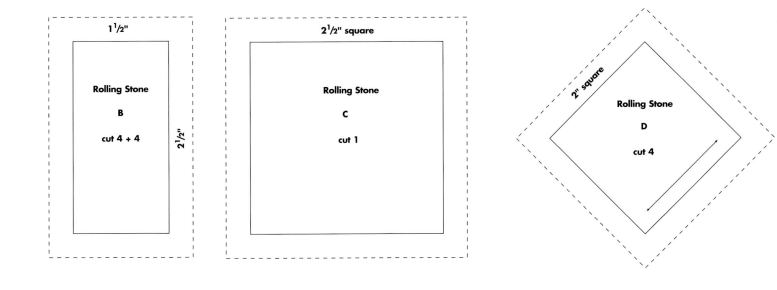

1½"

Rolling Stone

B

cut 4 + 4

2½"

2½" square

Rolling Stone

C

cut 1

2" square

Rolling Stone

D

cut 4

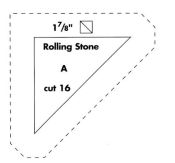

1⅞"

Rolling Stone

A

cut 16

HELPFUL HINTS

With this block, "less is more." Alternate with plain blocks to give it room to breathe.

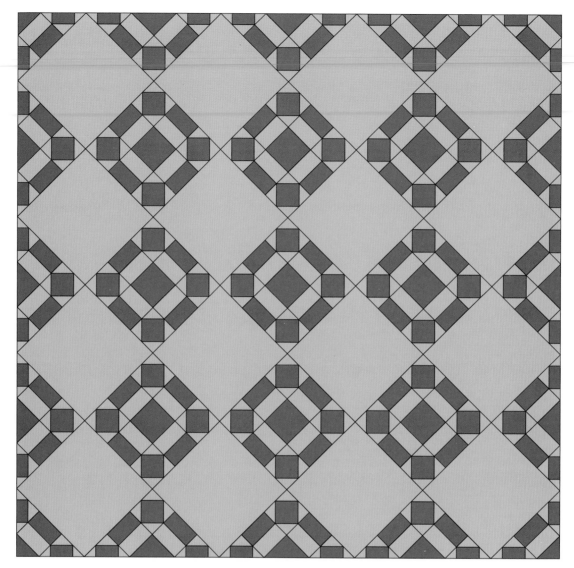

Rolling Stone 1727a

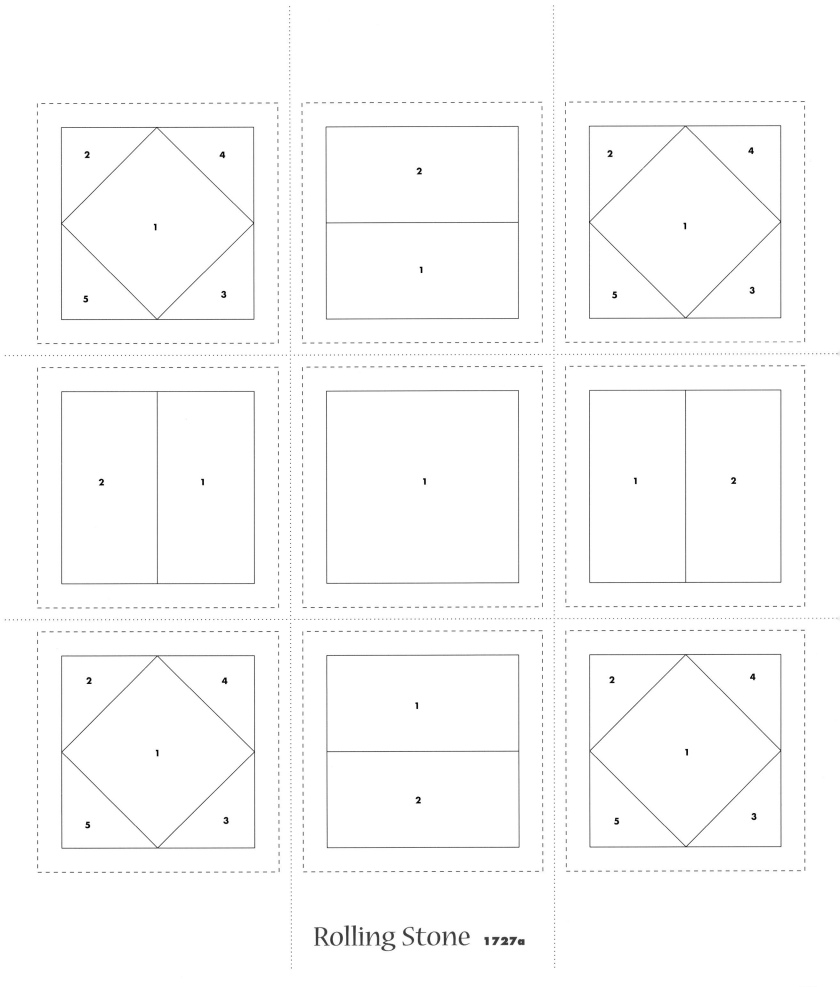

Rolling Stone 1727a

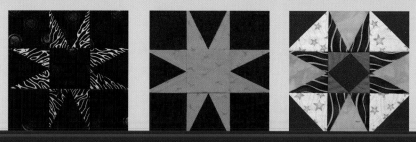

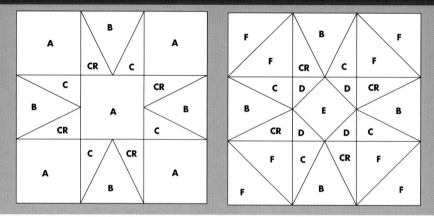

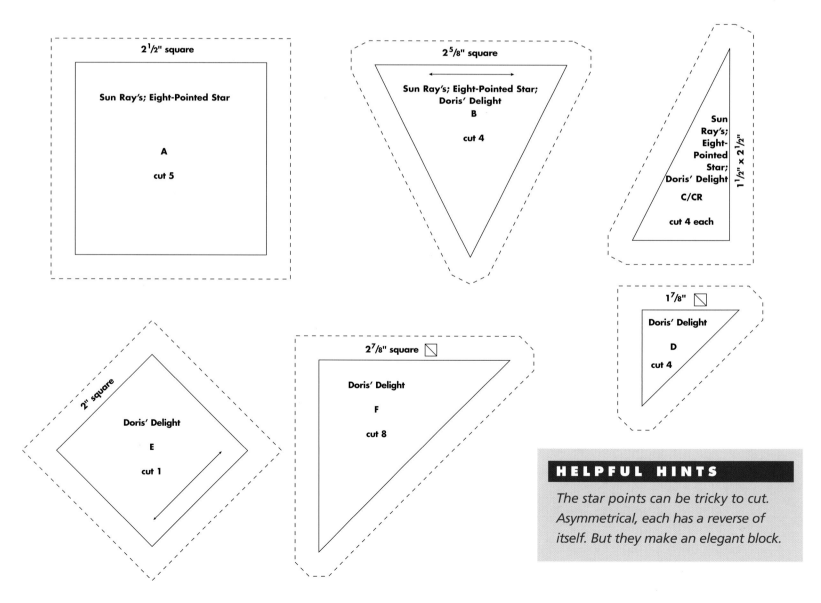

2½" square

Sun Ray's; Eight-Pointed Star

A

cut 5

2⅝" square

Sun Ray's; Eight-Pointed Star; Doris' Delight

B

cut 4

Sun Ray's; Eight-Pointed Star; Doris' Delight

C/CR

cut 4 each

1½" x 2½"

1⅞"

Doris' Delight

D

cut 4

2" square

Doris' Delight

E

cut 1

2⅞" square

Doris' Delight

F

cut 8

HELPFUL HINTS

The star points can be tricky to cut. Asymmetrical, each has a reverse of itself. But they make an elegant block.

Sun Ray's Quilt; Eight-Pointed Star; Doris' Delight **1623; 1624; 1626**

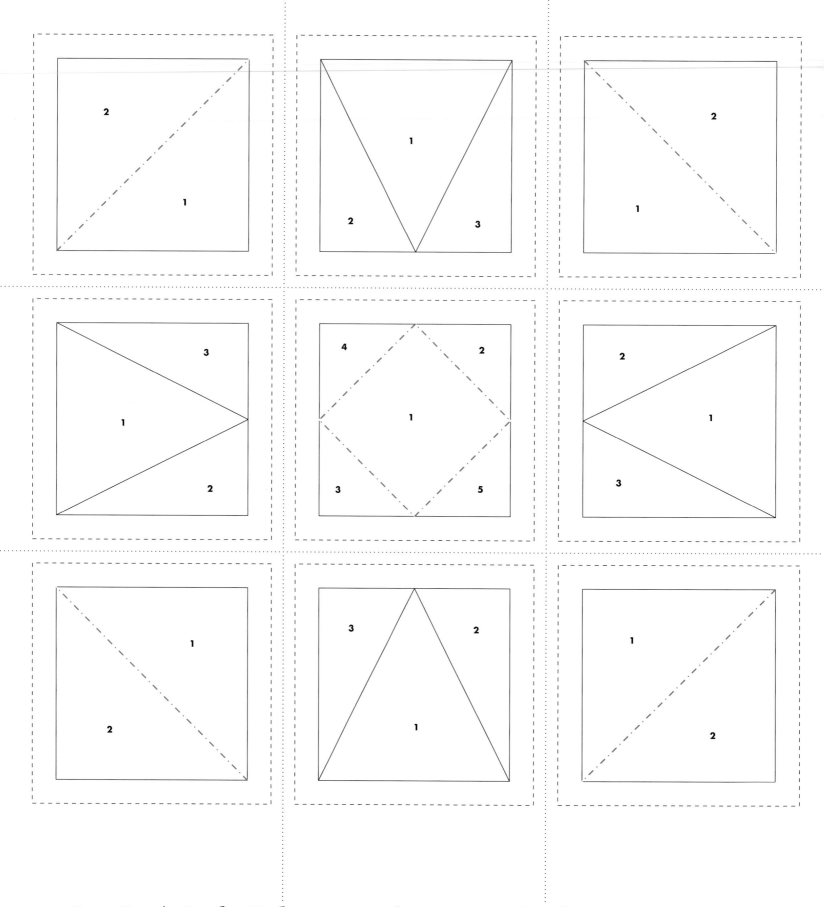

Sun Ray's Quilt; Eight-Pointed Star; Doris' Delight 1623; 1624; 1626

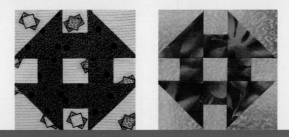

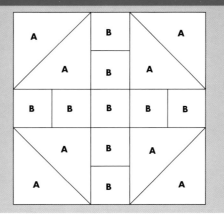

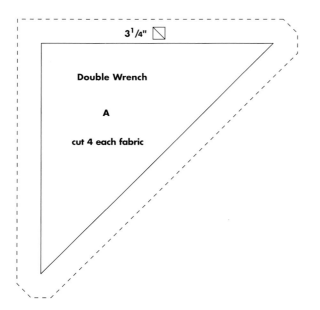

3¹/₄"

Double Wrench

A

cut 4 each fabric

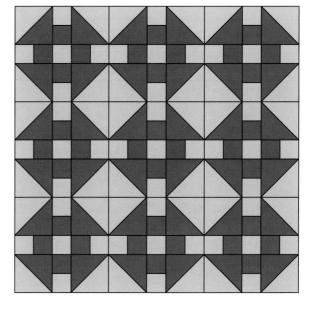

1³/₄" square

Double Wrench

B

cut 4 one fabric

cut 5 one fabric

HELPFUL HINTS

For the triangles, position and glue the lighter fabric down first, right side up, regardless of whether it is #1 or #2. The darker fabric will go right side down on top of the light triangle. This block looks great set on point with corner triangles (see page 123).

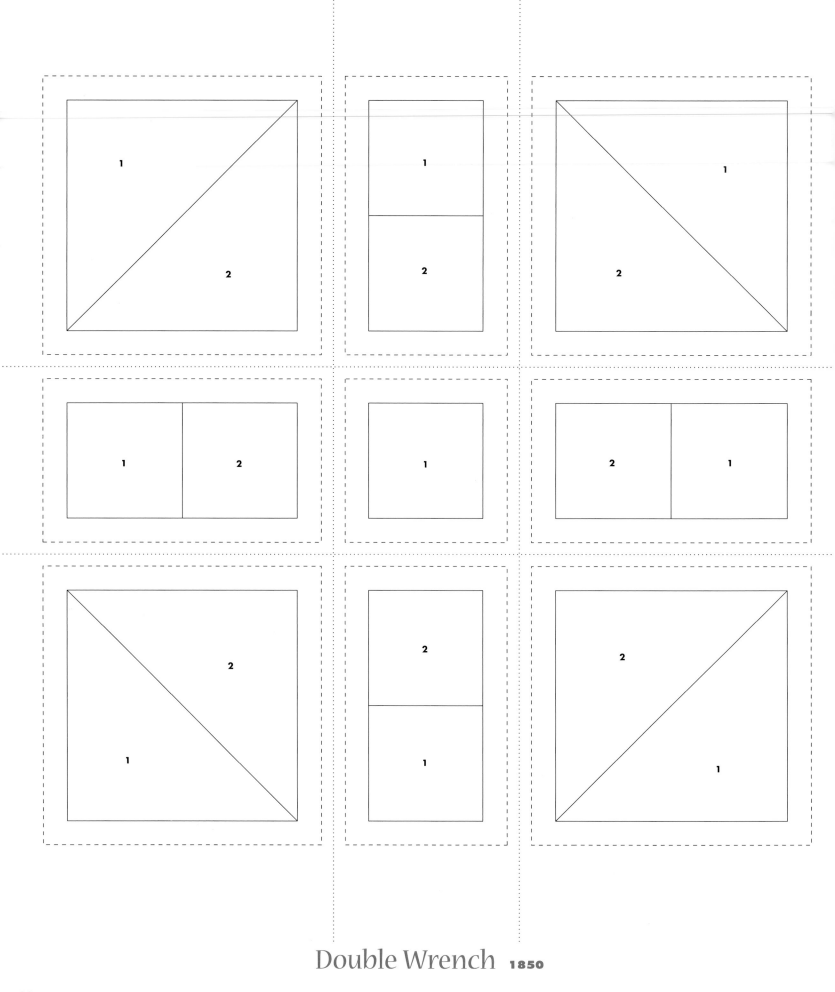

Double Wrench 1850

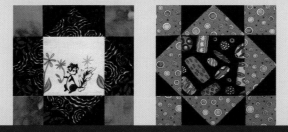

King's Crown 2039

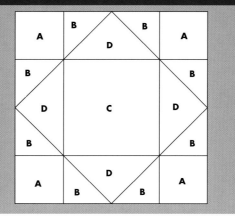

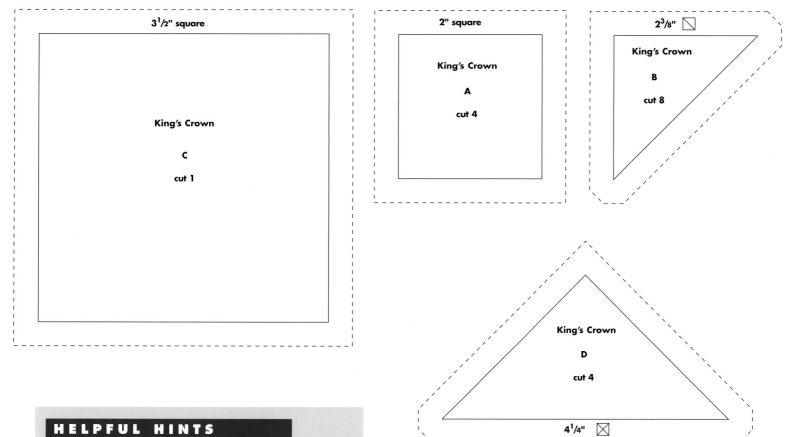

3¹/₂" square

King's Crown

C

cut 1

2" square

King's Crown

A

cut 4

2³/₈" ⊠

King's Crown

B

cut 8

King's Crown

D

cut 4

4¹/₄" ⊠

HELPFUL HINTS

The square in the center is a good place to feature a fabric photo transfer or a special motif.

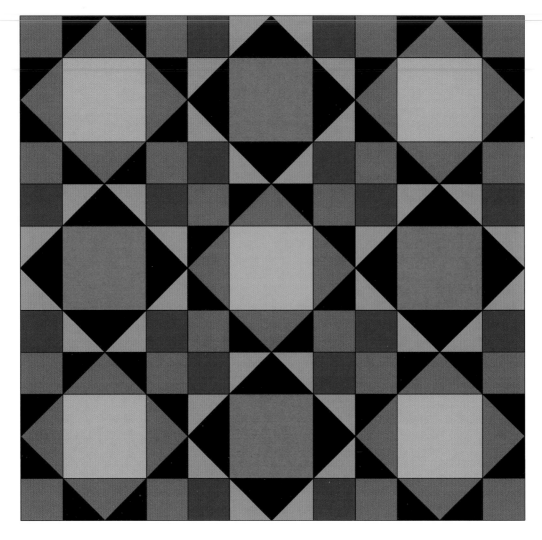

King's Crown **2039**

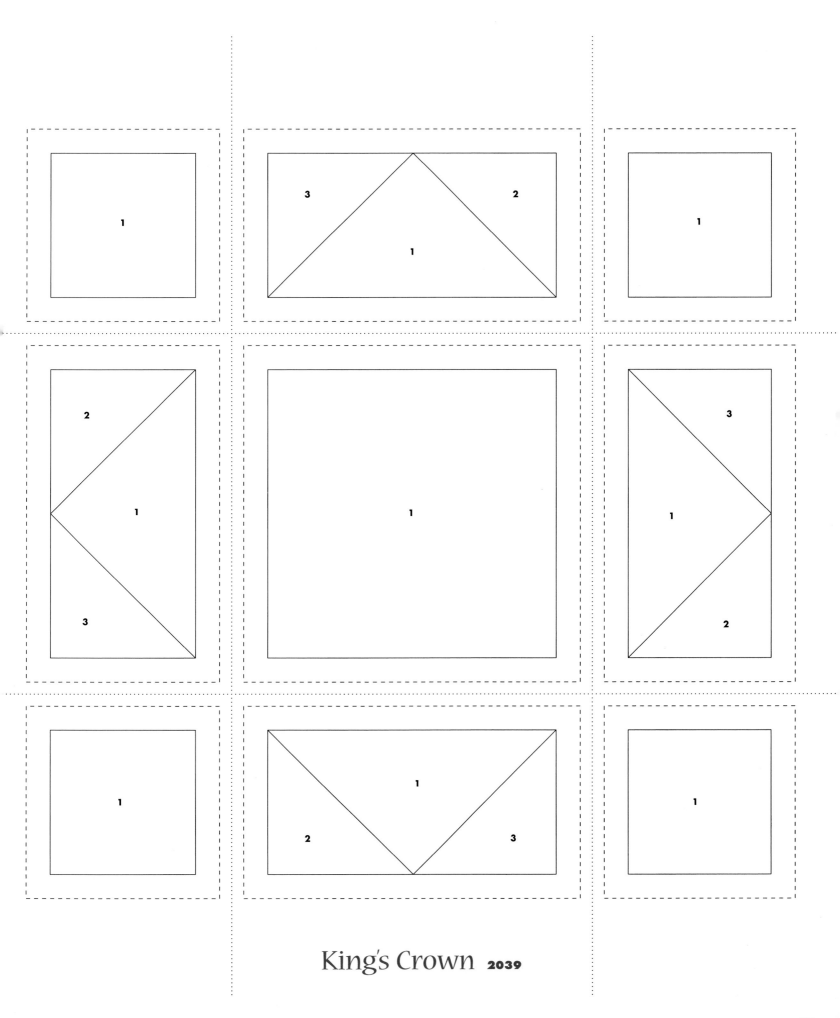

King's Crown 2039

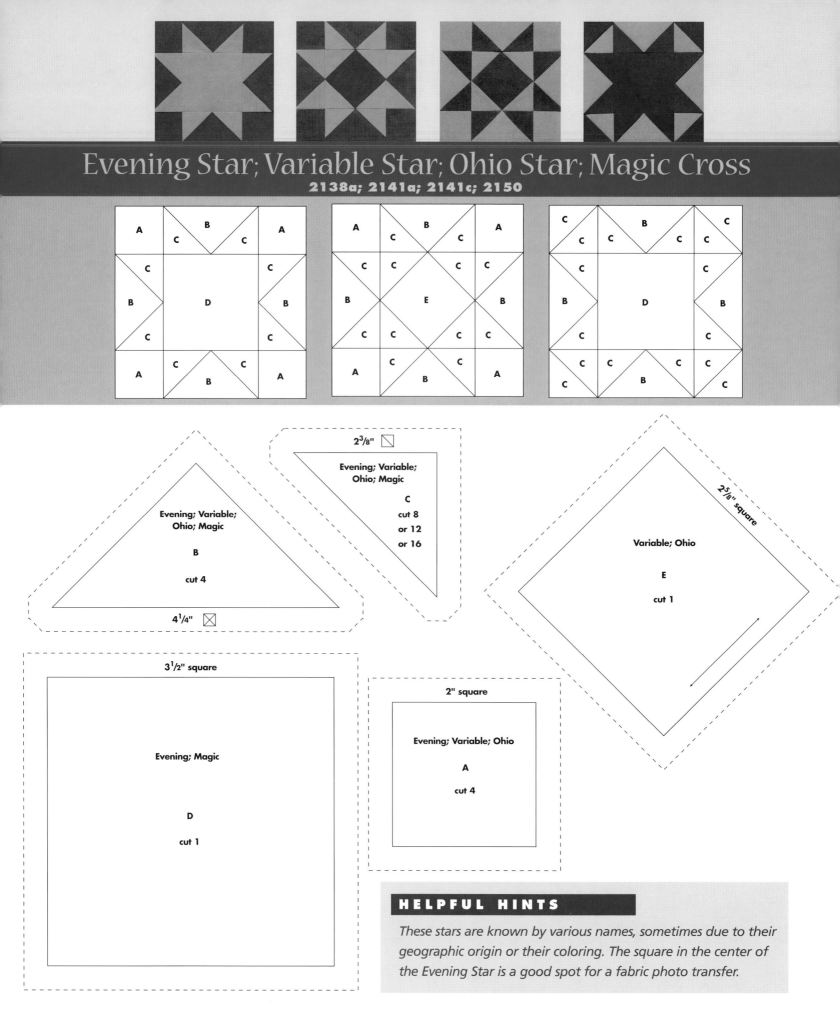

Evening Star; Variable Star; Ohio Star; Magic Cross
2138a; 2141a; 2141c; 2150

2³⁄₈" $\boxed{\diagup}$

Evening; Variable;
Ohio; Magic

C

cut 8
or 12
or 16

Evening; Variable;
Ohio; Magic

B

cut 4

4¹⁄₄" $\boxed{\times}$

2⁵⁄₈" square

Variable; Ohio

E

cut 1

3¹⁄₂" square

Evening; Magic

D

cut 1

2" square

Evening; Variable; Ohio

A

cut 4

HELPFUL HINTS

These stars are known by various names, sometimes due to their geographic origin or their coloring. The square in the center of the Evening Star is a good spot for a fabric photo transfer.

Ohio Star 2141c

Evening Star; Magic Cross Design *2138a; 2150*

Evening Star; Variable Star; Ohio Star; Magic Cross Design
2138a; 2141a; 2141c; 2150

Basket; Lady of the Lake   714 (modified); 707.5 (modified); K007

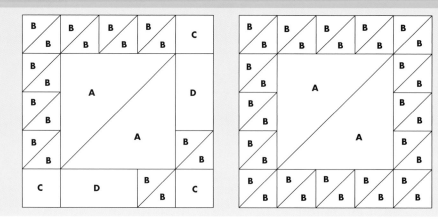

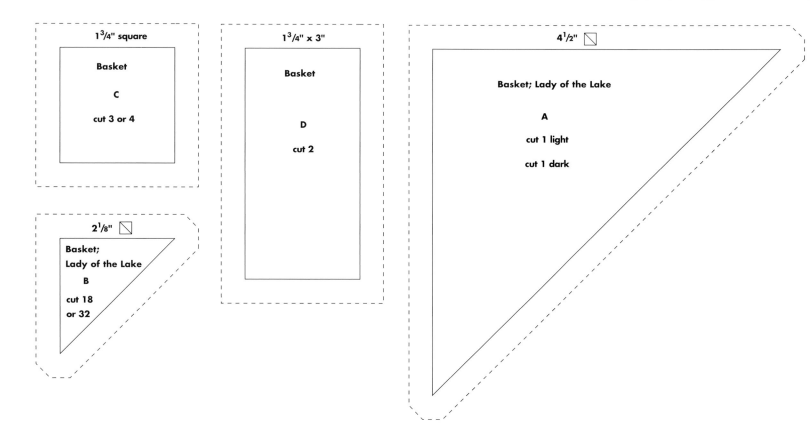

1³/₄" square

Basket

C

cut 3 or 4

1³/₄" x 3"

Basket

D

cut 2

4¹/₂" ◹

Basket; Lady of the Lake

A

cut 1 light

cut 1 dark

2¹/₈" ◹

Basket;
Lady of the Lake
B

cut 18
or 32

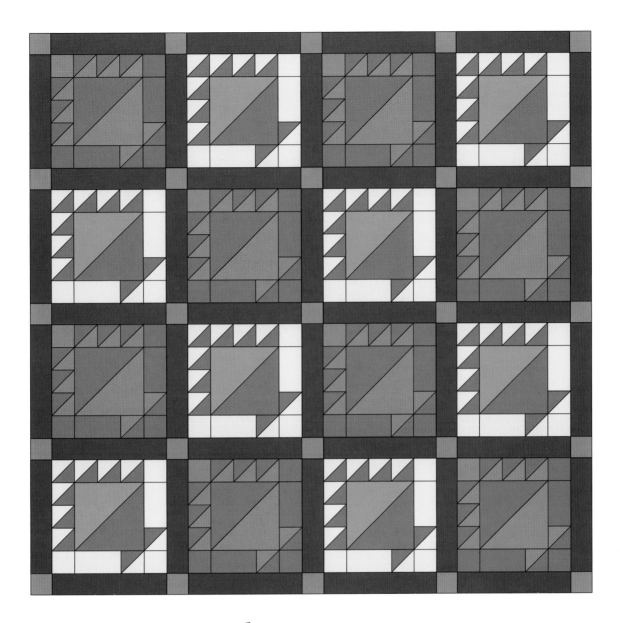

Basket 714 (modified); K007

These basket designs differ in the top left corner unit. Baskets are often set on point to "right" them, but setting blocks on point requires corner and side triangles, not as simple as setting them horizontally. Alternating these basket designs in a horizontal arrangement creates a nicely balanced quilt. The solid corner square of basket fabric in the top left corner of each block seems to "right" the quilt. It's a bit like straightening out the leaning tower of Pisa.

Lady of the Lake   707.5 (modified); K007

HELPFUL HINTS

My friend Susan Horn discovered the key to constructing the Lady of the Lake block. Pre cut all the triangles with the template and you'll have no trouble positioning them. Don't expect the triangles to always fill the seam allowances around the edges of the block. When the block is trued up, some of the foundation paper may be visible on the front. The paper edges of the block are aligned when you sew two blocks together.

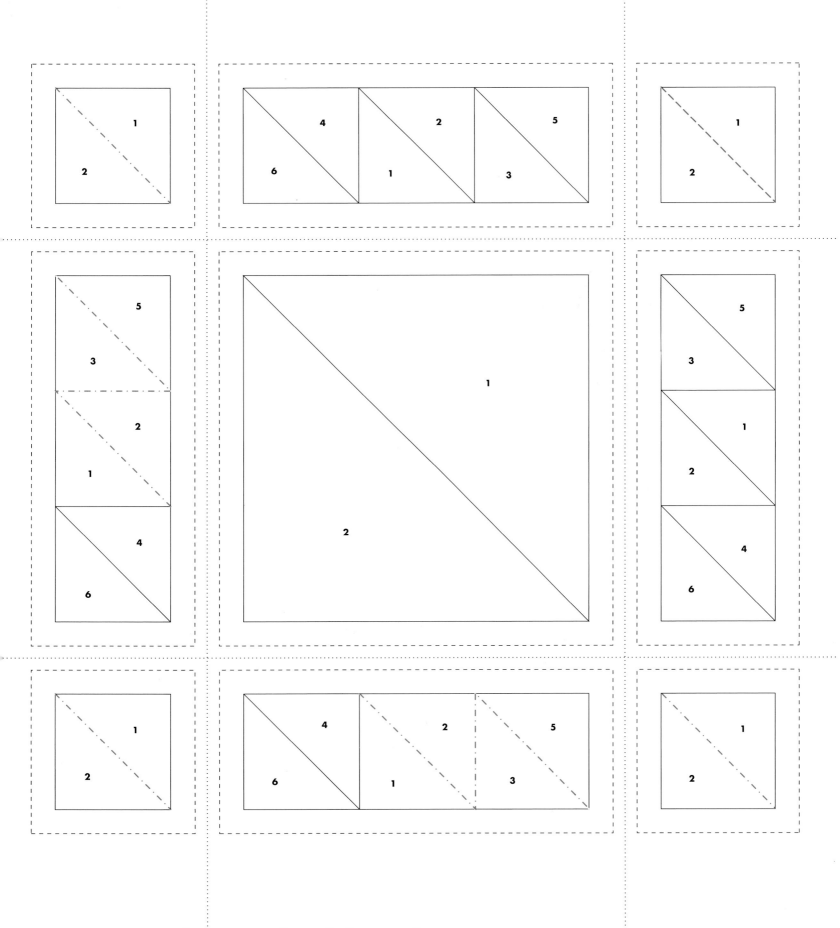

Baskets; Lady of the Lake 714 (modified); 707.5 (modified); K007

Palm 3174

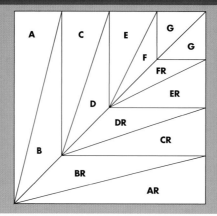

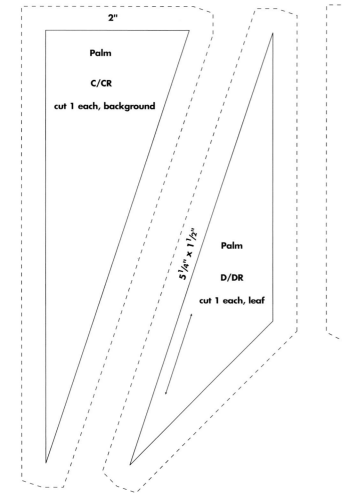

2"

Palm

C/CR

cut 1 each, background

Palm

D/DR

cut 1 each, leaf

5¼" × 1½"

2"

Palm

E/ER

cut 1 each,
background

Palm

F/FR

cut 1 each, leaf

3⅞" × 1¼"

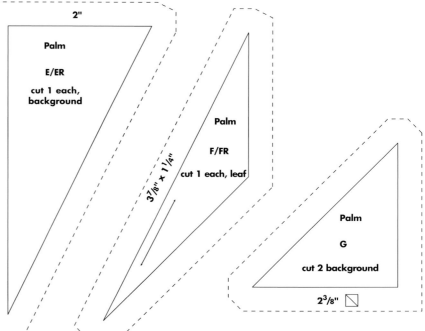

Palm

G

cut 2 background

2⅜"

HELPFUL HINTS

*My friend Pat McMahon recommends piecing from #1 to #7.
By sewing in this clockwise (or counterclockwise) order, the
seams will oppose each other when the long diagonal seam
is sewn and will lie perfectly against each other. This block
is best pieced from oversized strips of fabric rather than
templates. Just keep your fabric out of the gutter.*

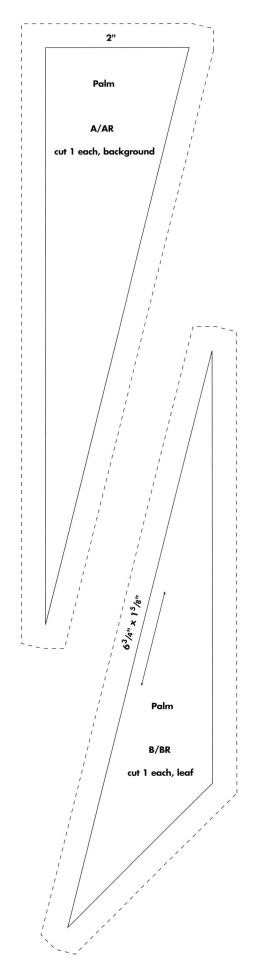

2"

Palm

A/AR

cut 1 each, background

6³/₄" x 1⁵/₈"

Palm

B/BR

cut 1 each, leaf

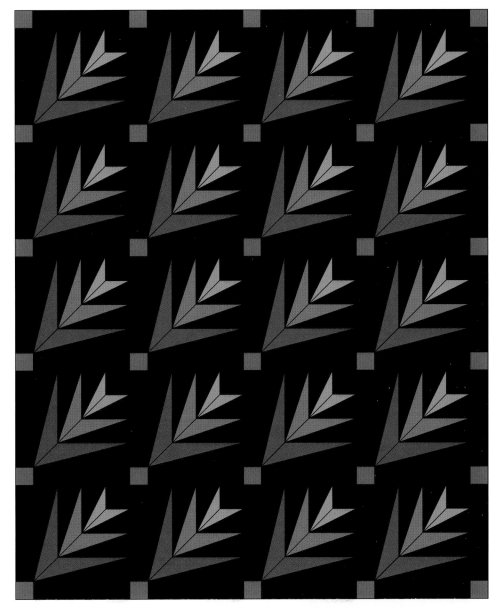

Palm 3174

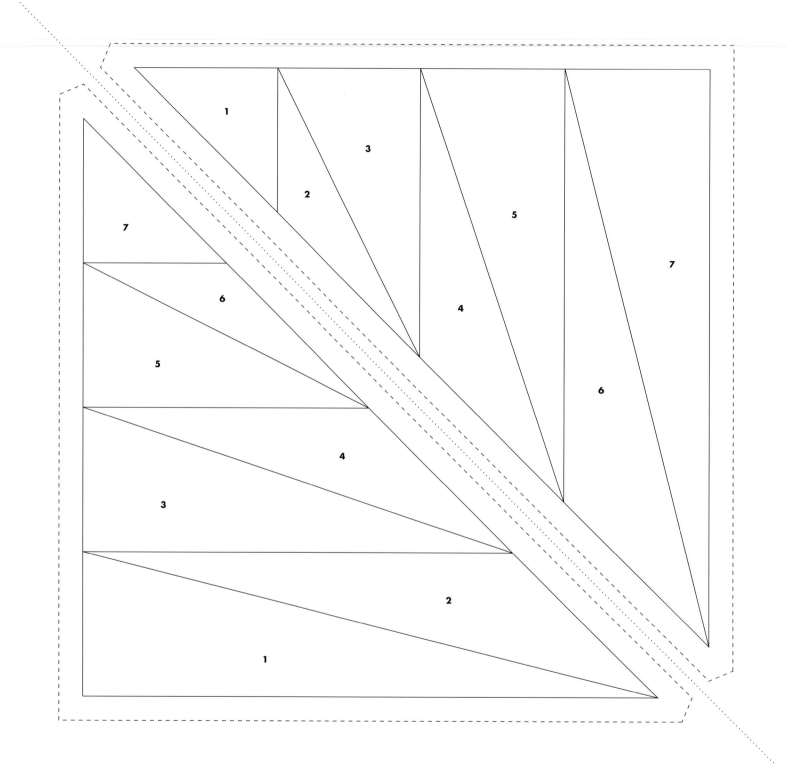

Palm 3174

Six-Pointed Star

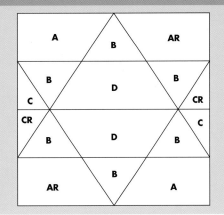

A	B	AR
B		B
C	D	CR
CR		C
B	D	B
AR	B	A

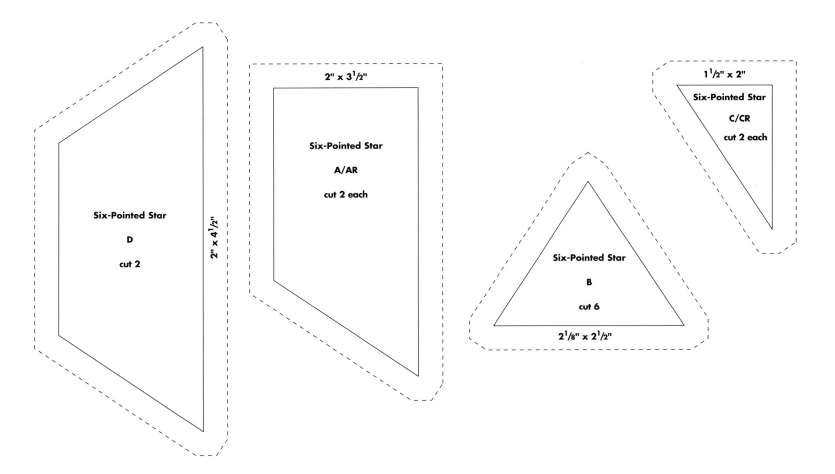

Six-Pointed Star

D

cut 2

2" x 4¹/₂"

2" x 3¹/₂"

Six-Pointed Star

A/AR

cut 2 each

Six-Pointed Star

B

cut 6

2¹/₈" x 2¹/₂"

1¹/₂" x 2"

Six-Pointed Star

C/CR

cut 2 each

Six-Pointed Star

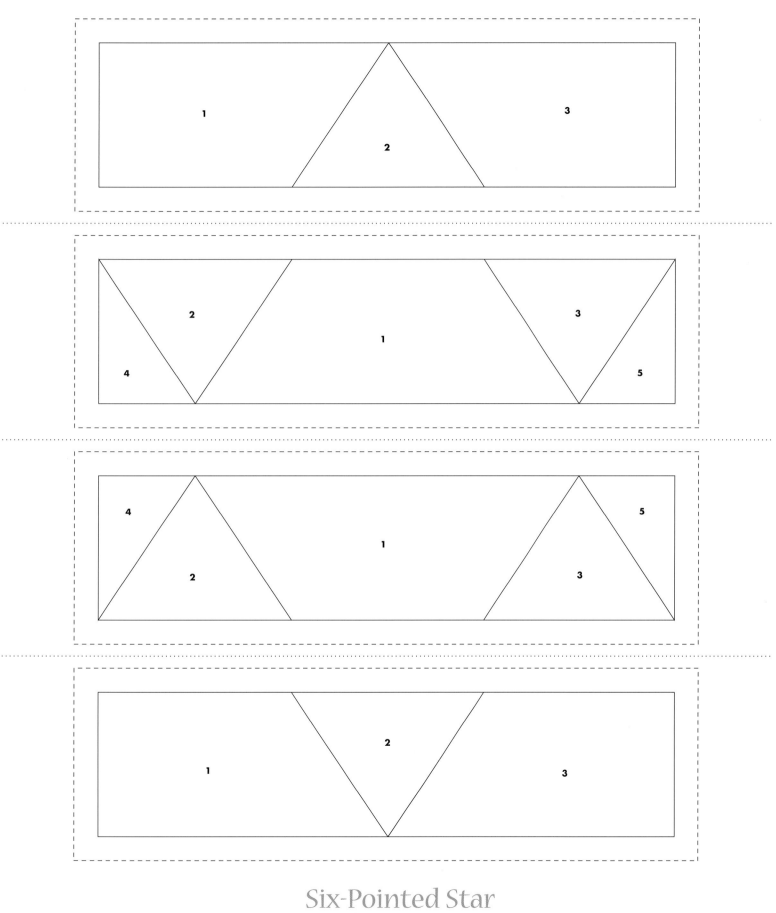

Six-Pointed Star

Chimney Sweep R010

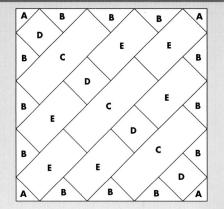

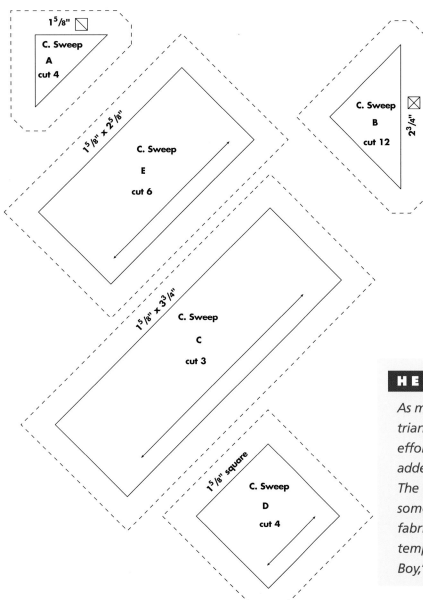

1 5/8" ⬜

C. Sweep
A
cut 4

1 5/8" x 2 5/8"

C. Sweep
E
cut 6

1 5/8" x 3 3/4"

C. Sweep
C
cut 3

1 5/8" square

C. Sweep
D
cut 4

C. Sweep
B
cut 12

2 3/4"

HELPFUL HINTS

As much as I loved the look of this block, the corner and side triangles were always a trial to sew on. It was a colossal effort to make a tidy block. The problem is solved now. An added bonus—the long parallel seams have no intersections. The Chimney Sweep is traditionally an autograph block and sometimes made with nineteenth century reproduction fabrics. Dorothea Hahn made these theme blocks with contemporary fabrics. Can you guess which is which? "It's a Boy," "Baby Shower," and "Retirement by the Sea?"

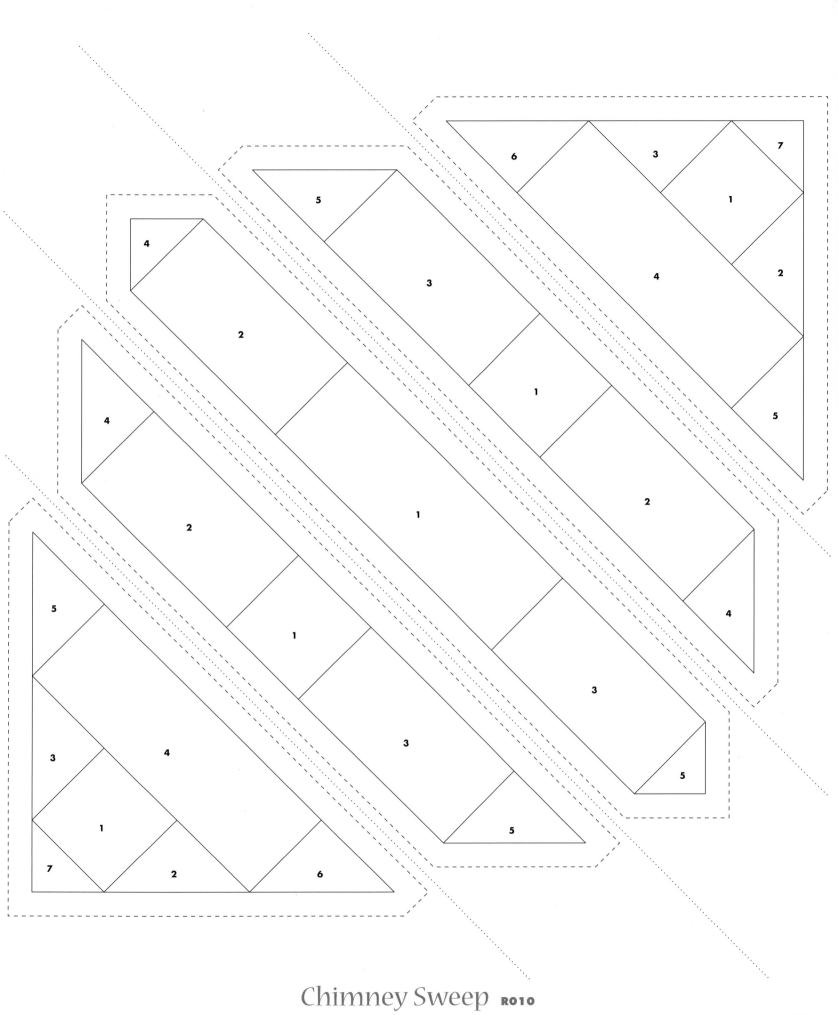

Chimney Sweep **RO10**

House on the Hill 826 (modified)

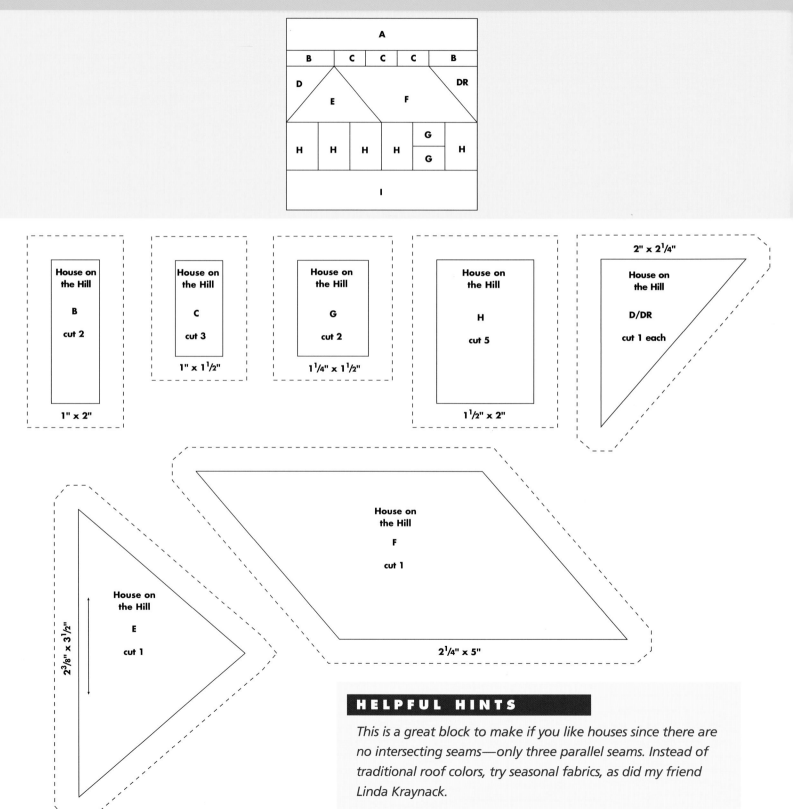

House on the Hill

B

cut 2

1" x 2"

House on the Hill

C

cut 3

1" x 1½"

House on the Hill

G

cut 2

1¼" x 1½"

House on the Hill

H

cut 5

1½" x 2"

House on the Hill

D/DR

cut 1 each

2" x 2¼"

House on the Hill

E

cut 1

2³/8" x 3½"

House on the Hill

F

cut 1

2¼" x 5"

HELPFUL HINTS

This is a great block to make if you like houses since there are no intersecting seams—only three parallel seams. Instead of traditional roof colors, try seasonal fabrics, as did my friend Linda Kraynack.

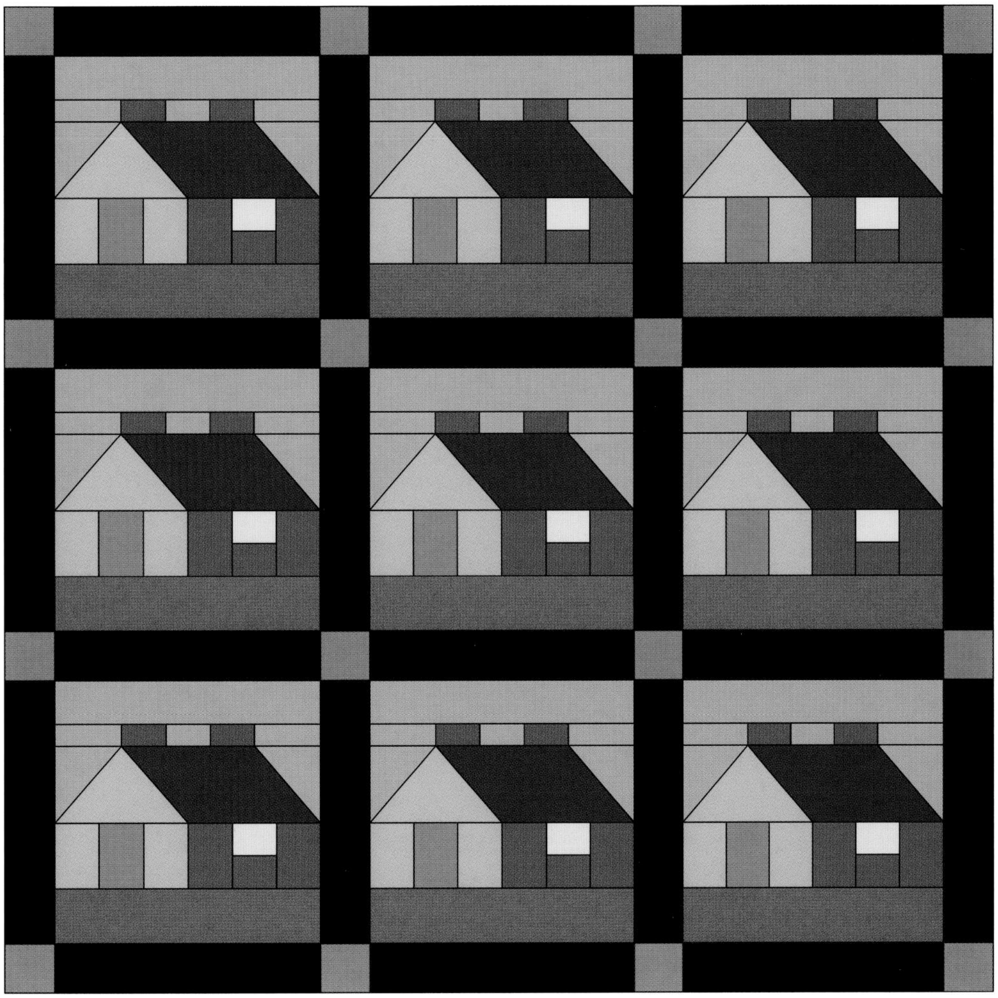

House on the Hill 826 (modified)

House on the Hill

I

cut 1

$1^3/4" \times 6^1/2"$

House on the Hill

A

cut 1

$1^1/2" \times 6^1/2"$

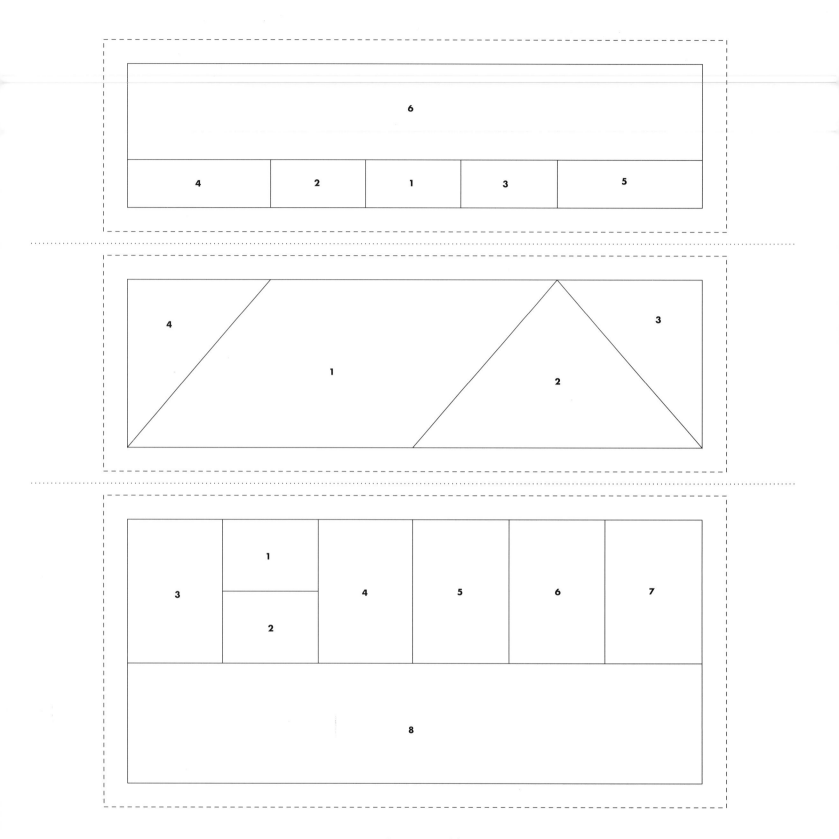

House on the Hill 826 (modified)

Eighteen Geese

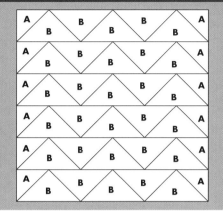

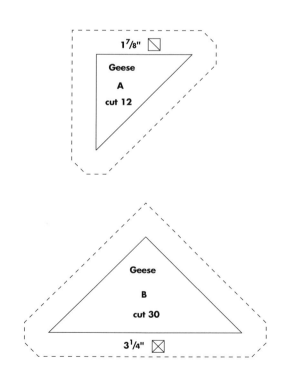

1⅞" ⬚

Geese
A
cut 12

Geese
B
cut 30

3¼" ⊠

Eighteen Geese

HELPFUL HINTS

For ease in construction, use the templates to cut the triangles. Note there are only five horizontal, non-intersecting seams. There are no vertical seams in this block requiring you to match points.

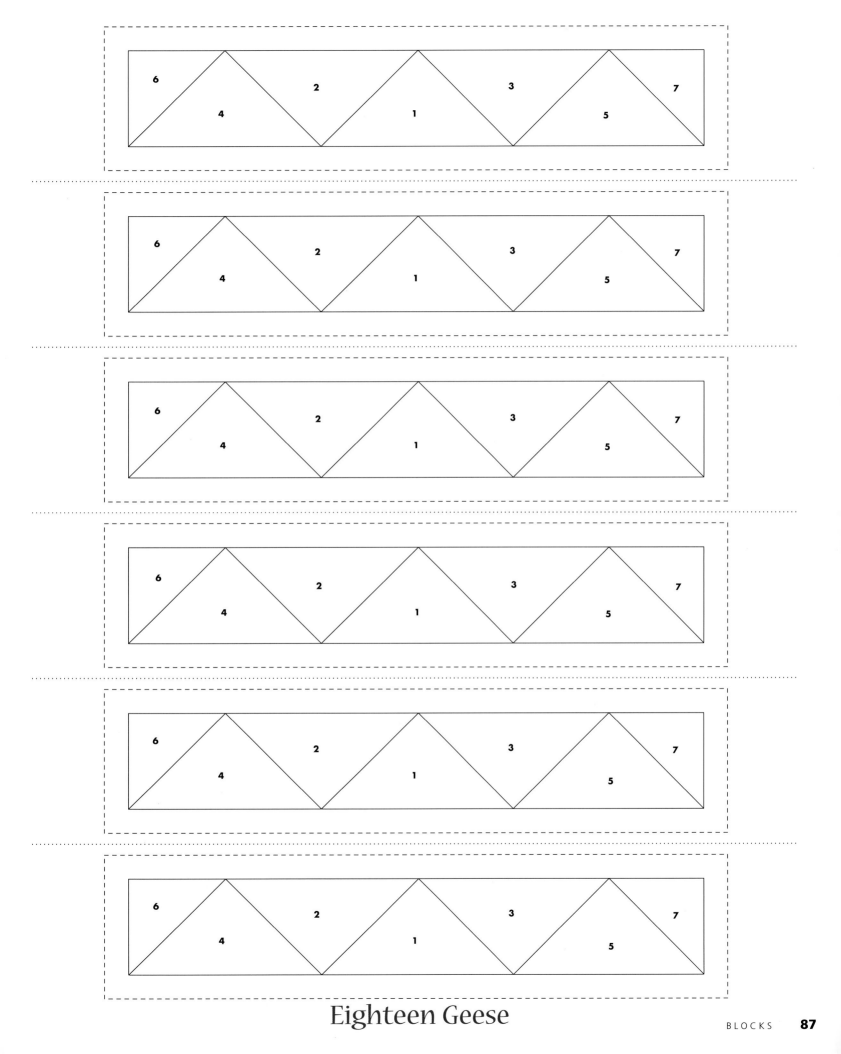

Eighteen Geese

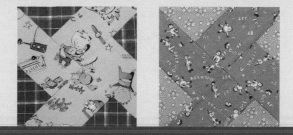

Twin Sisters 2314

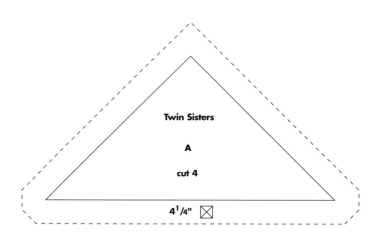

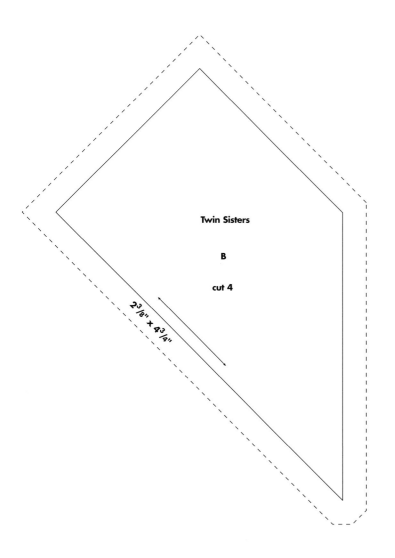

Twin Sisters

B

cut 4

2 3/8" x 4 3/4"

Twin Sisters

A

cut 4

4 1/4"

HELPFUL HINTS

This block goes together very quickly. Appropriately, the quilt shown is made by twin sisters, Emily and Barbara, working together. Also known as the Windmill and the Pinwheel, the Twin Sisters block was published by The Ladies Art Company of St. Louis around 1895.

Twin Sisters, made by Barbara Shuff Feinstein, Stamford, CT and twin sister Emily Shuff Klainberg, NY, NY.

Twin Sisters *2314*

Jan's Star 2345 (modified)

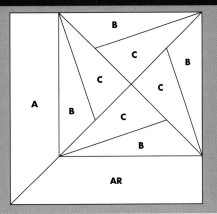

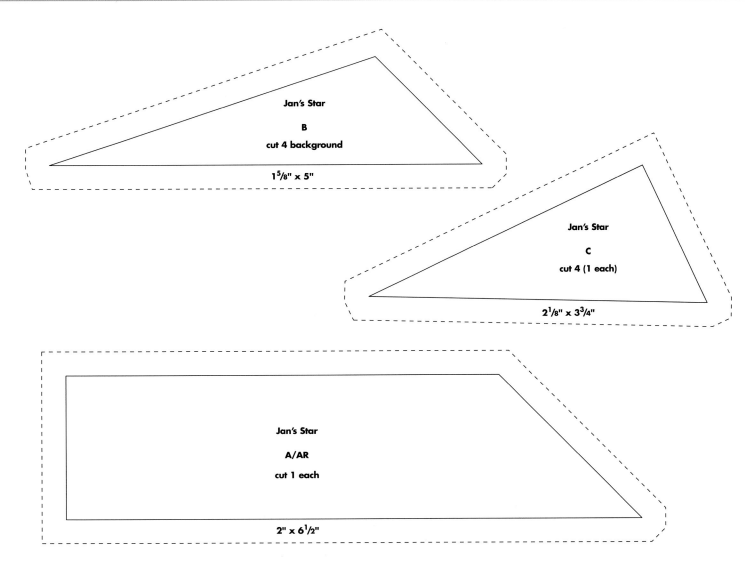

Jan's Star

B

cut 4 background

1⁵/₈" x 5"

Jan's Star

C

cut 4 (1 each)

2¹/₈" x 3³/₄"

Jan's Star

A/AR

cut 1 each

2" x 6¹/₂"

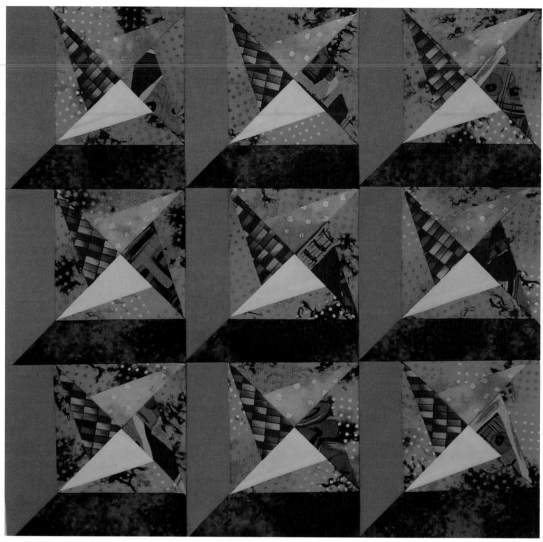

Jan's Star, made by Arlene Jacobs.

Cutting the fabric for this block requires concentration. It's economical and efficient to cut these pieces from long strips of fabric pre cut to the width specified on the template. If you layer the strips, keep the fabric right side up since the templates are asymmetrical. Be sure to keep the templates right side up although they can be rotated when cutting to use every last scrap of fabric. Remember that AR is A reversed. As with all reverse templates, take care not to mistake one for the other. Label your templates with a description of the fabric you will be using. Consider using a reversible fabric such as a batik. Then if you accidentally reverse your template while cutting, you can simply use the flip side.

Piecing this block is easy. It only takes two diagonal seams to join the subunits. Be sure the pieces are lightly glued in place before sewing the longest seam. Press the first seam, clip the intersection, and sew the remaining seam.

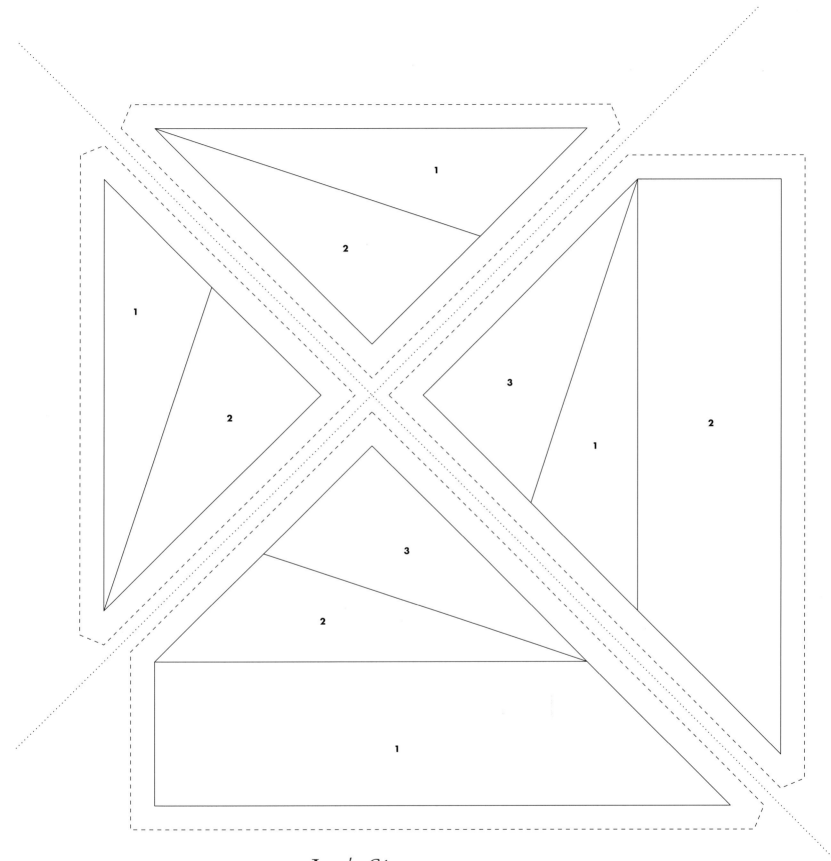

Jan's Star   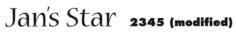   2345 (modified)

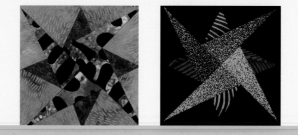

Starry Path *2346*

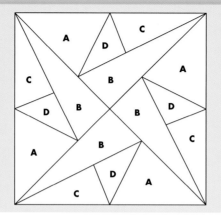

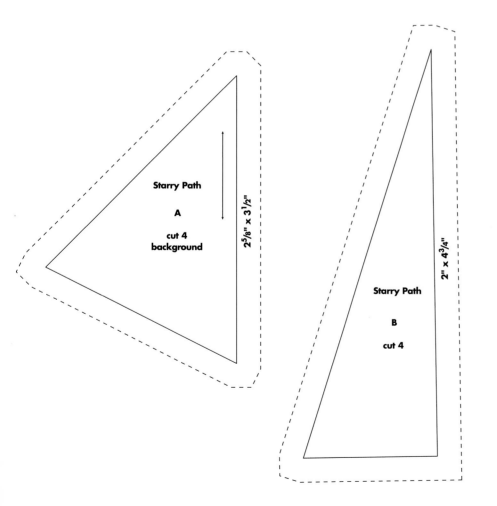

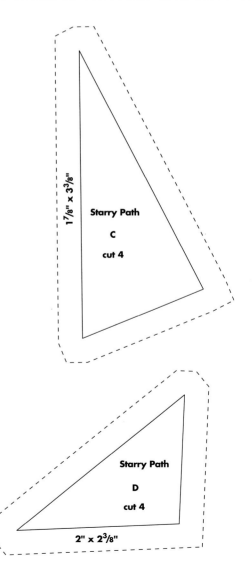

Starry Path

A

cut 4
background

$2^5/8" \times 3^1/2"$

Starry Path

B

cut 4

$2" \times 4^3/4"$

$1^7/8" \times 3^3/8"$

Starry Path

C

cut 4

Starry Path

D

cut 4

$2" \times 2^3/8"$

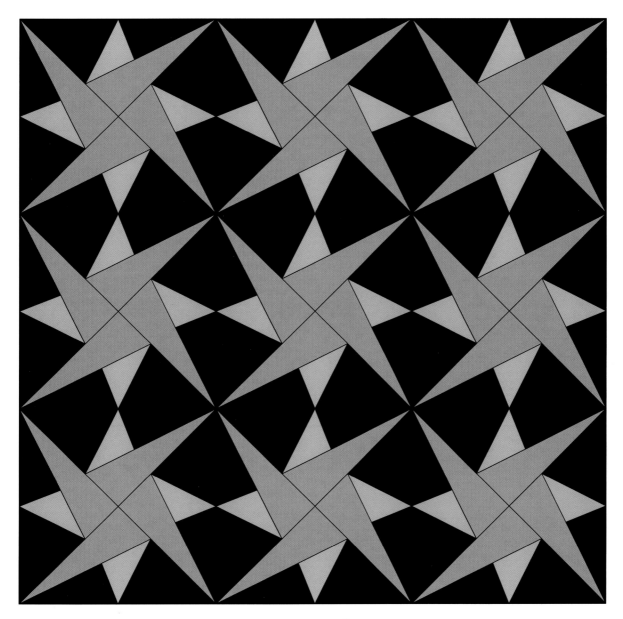

Starry Path 2346

Starry Path 2346

Zegart

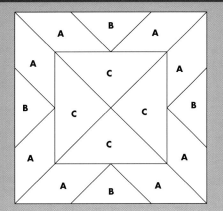

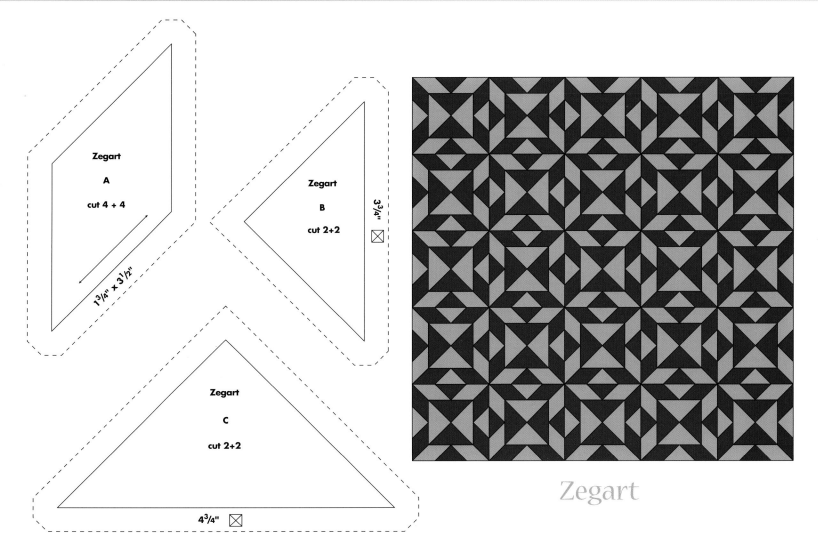

Zegart

Zegart

A

cut 4 + 4

1³/₄" x 3¹/₂"

Zegart

B

cut 2+2

3³/₄" ⊠

Zegart

C

cut 2+2

4³/₄" ⊠

Zegart

The Range's Pride 2341.5

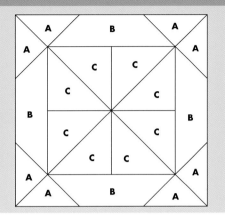

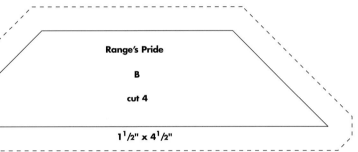

Range's Pride

B

cut 4

$1^1/2$" x $4^1/2$"

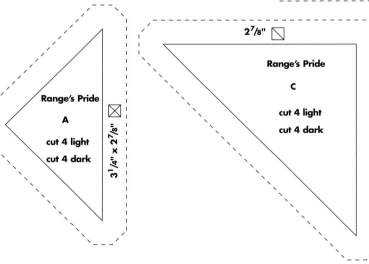

Range's Pride

A

cut 4 light

cut 4 dark

$3^1/4$" x $2^7/8$"

$2^7/8$"

Range's Pride

C

cut 4 light

cut 4 dark

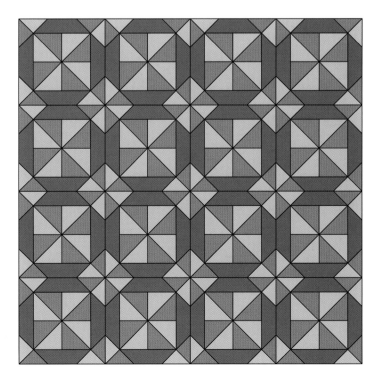

HELPFUL HINTS

To add the appearance of motion to the block, choose a darker fabric for the downward pointing "A" triangle in the upper right-hand corner (and it's three corresponding mates) then the adjacent "A" triangles. The block will appear to spin counter-clockwise.

The Range's Pride 2341.5

Faux Card Trick 1704 Air Castle (modified)

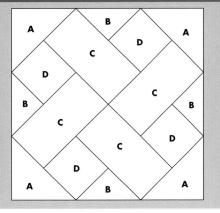

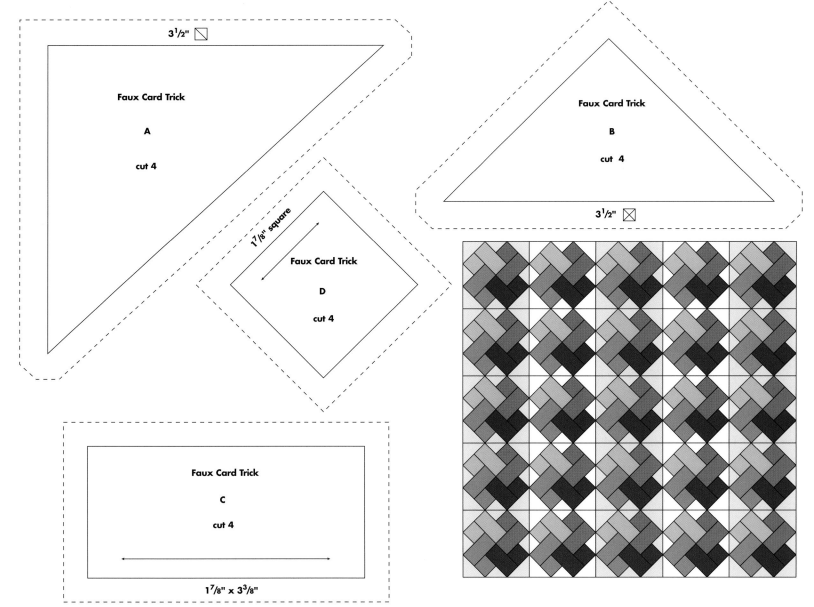

3½" ☐

Faux Card Trick

A

cut 4

1⅞" square

Faux Card Trick

B

cut 4

3½" ☒

Faux Card Trick

D

cut 4

Faux Card Trick

C

cut 4

1⅞" x 3⅜"

1. Choose card fabrics so the seams that join the squares and rectangles will not be noticeable. Each card is composed of one square and one rectangle of the same fabric. The square goes in one subunit but its rectangle goes across the gutter into the adjoining subunit.

These fabrics are too unevenly colored making the squares and rectangles obvious.

This block has the fabrics in the wrong subunits.

2. Piece everything except the corner triangles. Sew the two diagonal long seams to join the four subunits.

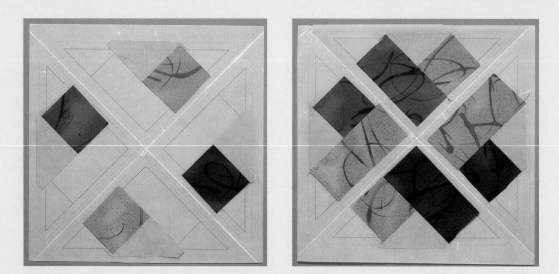

Both triangle background templates are intentionally oversized (to simplify construction and ease cutting). The B triangles are glued first and should extend ¹/₄" into the C & D area. Their bases should amply fill the seam allowances on the outside of the block. Triangle A, the last patch, is oversized to compensate for the bias and to allow generous seam allowances. "A" is a half-square triangle, "B" is a quarter square triangle and both are cut from 3¹/₂" squares.

3. *Attach the four outside triangles but don't stitch the flap down.*

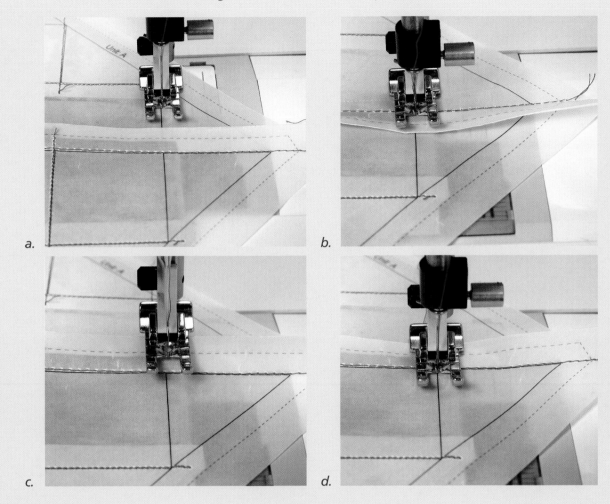

a.

b.

c.

d.

4. *Press the block open.*

Faux Card Trick **1704 Air Castle (modified)**

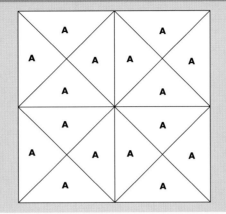

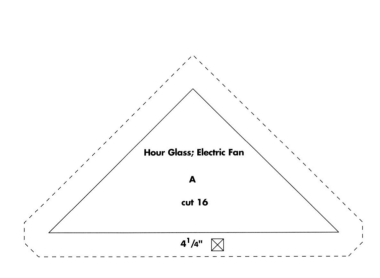

Hour Glass; Electric Fan

A

cut 16

4¹/₄"

HELPFUL HINTS

The fabric placement makes the difference in these two blocks. In the old days, I would have pieced four quarter-square units, pressed, trimmed, pinned, and joined them. Now I breeze through construction of this block.

Electric Fan 1195b

Hour Glass, Electric Fan 1195a, 1195b

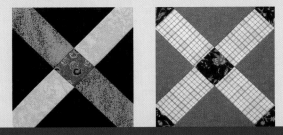

Old Italian Block; Crossroads 2881; 2883

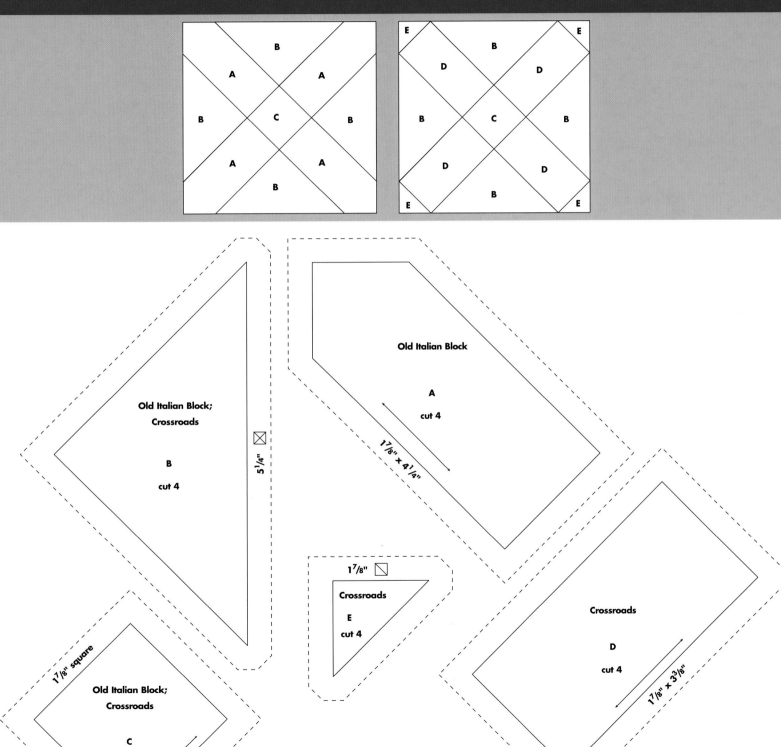

Old Italian Block;
Crossroads

B

cut 4

5¹⁄₄"

Old Italian Block

A

cut 4

1⁷⁄₈" × 4¹⁄₄"

1⁷⁄₈" square

Old Italian Block;
Crossroads

C

cut 1

1⁷⁄₈"

Crossroads

E

cut 4

Crossroads

D

cut 4

1⁄₈" × 3³⁄₈"

Old Italian Block; Crossroads 2881; 2883

HELPFUL HINTS

Make It Simpler—use a glue stick for the Old Italian Block. Just glue ALL of the subunits in place and sew up the seams. Voila! Crossroads requires the combined #1 #2 units be sewn to foundation before gluing the remaining pieces in place.

Old Italian Block; Crossroads *2881; 2883*

1904 Star 2795

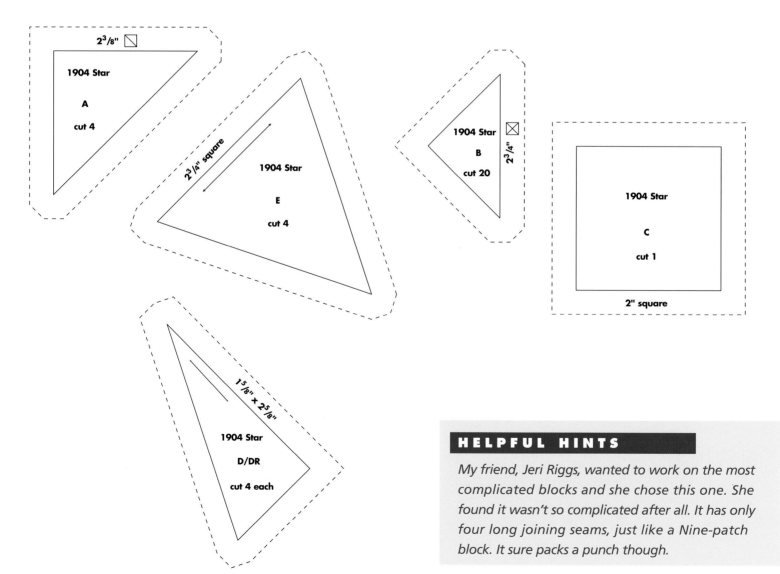

HELPFUL HINTS

My friend, Jeri Riggs, wanted to work on the most complicated blocks and she chose this one. She found it wasn't so complicated after all. It has only four long joining seams, just like a Nine-patch block. It sure packs a punch though.

1904 Star **2795**

1904 Star *2795*

Rambler 2795

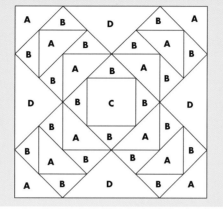

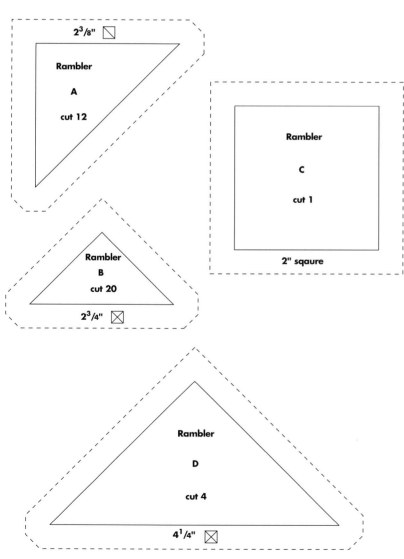

2³/₈" ⊠

Rambler

A

cut 12

Rambler

C

cut 1

2" sqaure

Rambler

B

cut 20

2³/₄" ⊠

Rambler

D

cut 4

4¹/₄" ⊠

HELPFUL HINTS

I have always liked this block, but never took any pleasure when I had to join the nine separate units. Now I enjoy making this block!

Rambler 2795

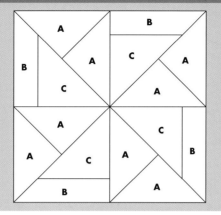

Pinwheel 1294

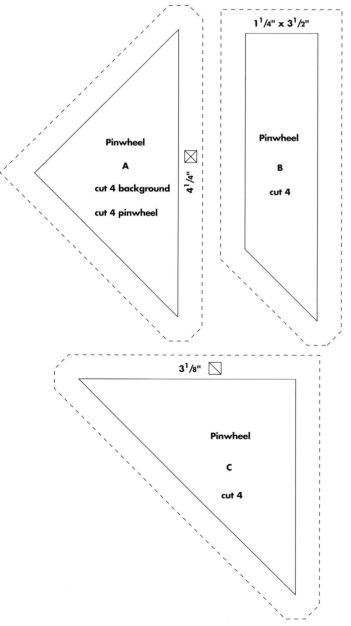

Pinwheel

A

cut 4 background

cut 4 pinwheel

1¹/₄" x 3¹/₂"

Pinwheel

B

cut 4

4¹/₄"

3¹/₈"

Pinwheel

C

cut 4

This Pinwheel, the Stauber Star, and the Hunter's Star have the same structure. Eight triangles converge at a single intersection in the center. Joining the subunits is the same for all three blocks. There are four long seams: one horizontal, one vertical, and two diagonal seams. The sewing of each is not continuous because you will jump over the seam allowances in the center of the block.

Sew the vertical seam from the outside edge toward the center of the block. When you reach the center of the block, stop sewing one stitch before the seam allowance point. Shorter stitches may give you more control. **Backstitch** and lift your needle. Resume sewing along the remainder of the vertical seam and off the edge of the block. Make the perpendicular clip and sew the horizontal seam in the same manner.

Sew either diagonal seam. Either begin sewing it at the edge of the block or in the center, whichever you prefer. After sewing the first half, trim away the excess paper in the center of the block, it just gets in your way. Don't trim any paper that has lines printed on it.

Clip the intersection. Sew the next diagonal seam. Clip the intersection. Press the block open.

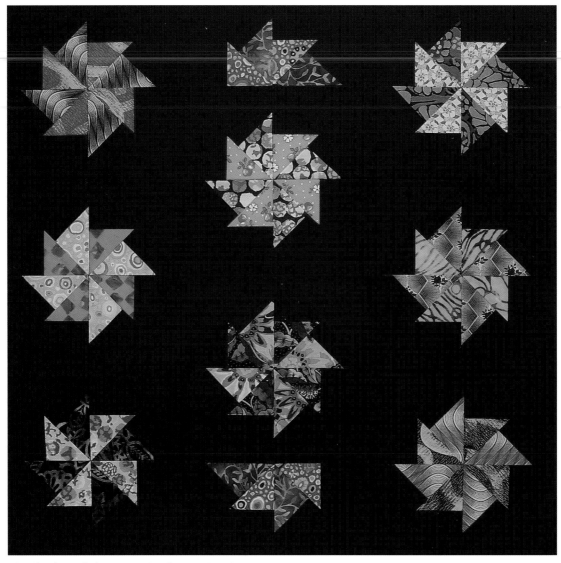

Pinwheel, made by Susan Stauber, NY, NY.

Grid indicates how blocks were set.

Pinwheel 1294

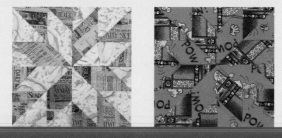

Stauber Star

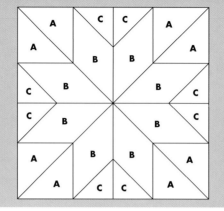

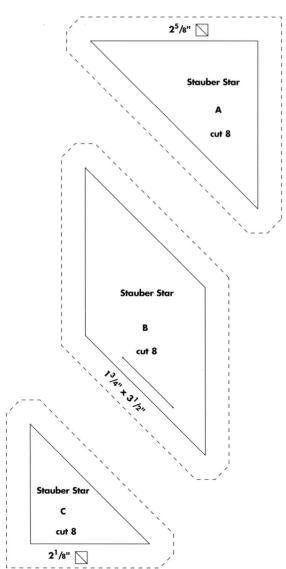

2⁵⁄₈" $\square$

Stauber Star

A

cut 8

Stauber Star

B

cut 8

1³⁄₄" × 3¹⁄₂"

Stauber Star

C

cut 8

2¹⁄₈" $\square$

HELPFUL HINTS

I will always be astonished by how easy it is with this method to make this eight-pointed star, without using a single pin or basting stitch. My friend, Susan Stauber, made hundreds of these in less than six months and they were breathtaking to see on a design wall. Which was the only time a pin ever touched them.

Stauber Star

Hunter's Star

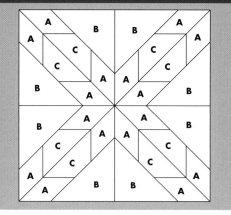

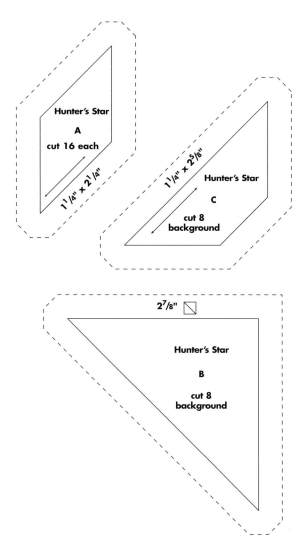

Hunter's Star
A
cut 16 each

$1^{1}/_{4}$" x $2^{1}/_{4}$"

$1^{1}/_{4}$" x $2^{5}/_{8}$"

Hunter's Star
C
cut 8
background

$2^{7}/_{8}$"

Hunter's Star
B
cut 8
background

Hunter's Star

Stella's Star made by Anita Grossman Solomon, NY, NY.

Hunter's Star

Corner Triangle, Churn Dash

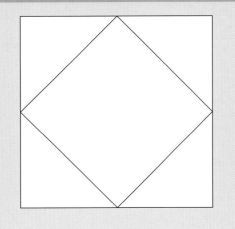

Adding a corner triangle is a great way to enlarge your block while giving it some breathing room in the quilt at the same time. A 6½" (6" finished) block can be set on point and turned into an 8½" (8" finished) block by adding corner triangles to each side of the block. Cut two 5½" squares of fabric, then cut each on the diagonal to get four oversize corner triangles.

Sew the long side of each triangle to opposite edges of the block. Press and then sew the remaining triangles onto the block.

Use an 8½" square ruler to true up your block after the triangles have been sewn to each side of the block.

HELPFUL HINTS

If you have a stripe, plaid or other directional fabric, place one square with the design vertically, and the second with the design horizontally right side up, on top of each other. Cut diagonally. The original orientation of the triangles is maintained when they are arranged around your block. Although I like the look of mismatched striped and plaid triangles, it's helpful to know how to have control over them.

Tom's Churn Dash, made by Anita Grossman Solomon, NY, NY. *This Churn Dash quilt was made by the author in 1997 and shows corner triangles setting a block on point. There is no pattern for the **Churn Dash** in this book, but the Double Wrench on page 61 is comparable.*

OTHER FINE BOOKS FROM C&T PUBLISHING

15 Two-Block Quilts: Unlock the Secrets of Secondary Patterns, Claudia Olson

24 Quilted Gems: Sparkling Traditional & Original Projects, Gai Perry

All About Quilting from A to Z, From the Editors and Contributors of Quilter's Newsletter Magazine and Quiltmaker Magazine

America from the Heart: Quilters Remember September 11, 2001, Karey Bresenhan

An Amish Adventure, 2nd Edition: A Workbook for Color in Quilts, Roberta Horton

Art of Classic Quiltmaking, The, Harriet Hargrave & Sharyn Craig

At Piece With Time: A Woman's Journey Stitched in Cloth, Kristin Steiner & Diane Frankenberger

Beautifully Quilted with Alex Anderson: • How to Choose or Create the Best Designs for Your Quilt • 5 Timeless Projects • Full-Size Patterns, Ready to Use, Alex Anderson

Block Magic: Over 50 Fun & Easy Blocks from Squares and Rectangles, Nancy Johnson-Srebro

Block Magic, Too!: Over 50 NEW Blocks from Squares and Rectangles, Nancy Johnson-Srebro

Bouquet of Quilts, A: Garden-Inspired Projects for the Home, Edited by Jennifer Rounds & Cyndy Lyle Rymer

Celebrate the Tradition with C&T Publishing: Over 70 Fabulous New Blocks, Tips & Stories from Quilting's Best, C&T Staff

Civil War Women: Their Quilts, Their Roles & Activities for Re-Enactors, Barbara Brackman

Color from the Heart: Seven Great Ways to Make Quilts with Colors You Love, Gai Perry

Color Play: Easy Steps to Imaginative Color in Quilts, Joen Wolfrom

Contemporary Classics in Plaids & Stripes: 9 Projects from Piece 'O Cake Designs, Linda Jenkins & Becky Goldsmith

Cotton Candy Quilts: Using Feed Sacks, Vintage, and Reproduction Fabrics, Mary Mashuta

Cut-Loose Quilts: Stack, Slice, Switch, and Sew, Jan Mullen

Easy Pieces: Creative Color Play with Two Simple Quilt Blocks, Margaret Miller

Endless Possibilities: Using No-Fail Methods, Nancy Johnson-Srebro

Exploring Machine Trapunto: New Dimensions, Hari Walner

Fabric Shopping with Alex Anderson, Alex Anderson

Fabric Stamping Handbook, The: • Fun Projects • Tips & Tricks • Unlimited Possibilities, Jean Ray Laury

Fantastic Fabric Folding: Innovative Quilting Projects, Rebecca Wat

Fantastic Fans: Exquisite Quilts & Other Projects, Alice Dunsdon

Fast, Fun & Easy Fabric Bowls: 5 Reversible Shapes to Use & Display, Linda Johanson

Felt Wee Folk: Enchanting Projects, Salley Mavor

Floral Affair, A: Quilts & Accessories for Romantics, Nihon Vogue

Flowering Favorites from Piece O' Cake Designs: Becky Goldsmith & Linda Jenkins

Freddy's House: Brilliant Color in Quilts, Freddy Moran

Free Stuff for Quilters on the Internet, 3rd Edition, Judy Heim & Gloria Hansen

Free Stuff for Sewing Fanatics on the Internet, Judy Heim & Gloria Hansen

Free Stuff for Stitchers on the Internet, Judy Heim & Gloria Hansen

Free Stuff for Traveling Quilters on the Internet, Gloria Hansen

Free-Style Quilts: A "No Rules" Approach, Susan Carlson

Garden-Inspired Quilts: Design Journals for 12 Quilt Projects, Jean & Valori Wells

Hand Appliqué with Alex Anderson: Seven Projects for Hand Appliqué, Alex Anderson

Hand Quilting with Alex Anderson: Six Projects for First-Time Hand Quilters, Alex Anderson

Heirloom Machine Quilting, Third Edition: Comprehensive Guide to Hand-Quilting Effects Using Your Sewing Machine, Harriet Hargrave

Hidden Block Quilts: • Discover New Blocks Inside Traditional Favorites • 13 Quilt Settings • Instructions for 76 Blocks, Lerlene Nevaril

Hunter Star Quilts & Beyond: Jan Krentz

Imagery on Fabric, Second Edition: A Complete Surface Design Handbook, Jean Ray Laury

Kaleidoscope Artistry, Cozy Baker

Kaleidoscopes & Quilts, Paula Nadelstern

Kids Start Quilting with Alex Anderson: • 7 Fun & Easy Projects • Quilts for Kids by Kids • Tips for Quilting with Children, Alex Anderson

Laurel Burch Quilts: Kindred Creatures, Laurel Burch

Liberated String Quilts, Gwen Marston

Lone Star Quilts and Beyond: Step-by-Step Projects and Inspiration, Jan Krentz

Machine Embroidery and More: Ten Step-by-Step Projects Using Border Fabrics & Beads, Kristen Dibbs

Magical Four-Patch and Nine-Patch Quilts, Yvonne Porcella

Mariner's Compass Quilts: New Directions, Judy Mathieson

Mary Mashuta's Confetti Quilts: A No-Fuss Approach to Color, Fabric & Design, Mary Mashuta

Mastering Machine Appliqué, 2nd Edition: The Complete Guide Including: • Invisible Machine Appliqué • Satin Stitch • Blanket Stitch & Much More, Harriet Hargrave

Measure the Possibilities with Omnigrid®, Nancy Johnson-Srebro

Michael James: Art & Inspirations, Michael James

New England Quilt Museum Quilts, The: Featuring the Story of the Mill Girls, with Instructions for 5 Heirloom Quilts, Jennifer Gilbert

New Look at Log Cabin Quilts, A: Design a Scene Block by Block PLUS 10 Easy-to-Follow Projects, Flavin Glover

New Sampler Quilt, The, Diana Leone

On the Surface: Thread Embellishment & Fabric Manipulation, Wendy Hill

Paper Piecing Picnic: Fun-Filled Projects for Every Quilter, From the Editors and Contributors of *Quilter's Newsletter Magazine* and *Quiltmaker* magazine

Paper Piecing Potpourri: Fun-Filled Projects for Every Quilter, From the Editors and Contributors of *Quilter's Newsletter Magazine* and *Quiltmaker* magazine

Paper Piecing with Alex Anderson: • Tips • Techniques • 6 Projects, Alex Anderson

Patchwork Persuasion: Fascinating Quilts from Traditional Designs, Joen Wolfrom

Patchwork Quilts Made Easy—Revised, 2nd Edition: 33 Quilt Favorites, Old & New, Jean Wells

Perfect Union of Patchwork & Appliqué, A, Darlene Christopherson

Pieced Flowers, Ruth B. McDowell

Pieced Vegetables, Ruth B. McDowell

Piecing: Expanding the Basics, Ruth B. McDowell

Plentiful Possibilities: A Timeless Treasury of 16 Terrific Quilts, Lynda Milligan & Nancy Smith

Provence Quilts and Cuisine, Marie-Christine Flocard & Cosabeth Parriaud

Q is for Quilt, Diana McClun & Laura Nownes

Quick-Strip Paper Piecing: For Blocks, Borders & Quilts, Peggy Martin

Quilted Garden, The: Design & Make Nature-Inspired Quilts, Jane Sassaman

ABOUT THE AUTHOR

Anita Grossman Solomon is an award-winning quilter and quilting instructor who invented "Make It Simpler" techniques to make quilting faster and easier. She has a degree in art and began quilting more than a decade ago. Anita lives in New York City.

Anita Grossman Solomon can be contacted at
www.makeitsimpler.com

For more information, write for a free catalog:
C&T Publishing, Inc.
P.O. Box 1456
Lafayette, CA 94549
(800) 284-1114
Email: ctinfo@ctpub.com
Website: www.ctpub.com

For quilting supplies:
Cotton Patch Mail Order
3405 Hall Lane, Dept.CTB
Lafayette, CA 94549
(800) 835-4418
(925) 283-7883
Email:quiltusa@yahoo.com
Website: www.quiltusa.com

Note: Fabrics used in the quilts shown may not be currently available since fabric manufacturers keep most fabrics in print for only a short time.

CONTRIBUTING QUILTERS

 Alex Anderson

Beyond beginner

 Denise Bradley

A Mom who quilts to keep sane

 **Barbara Shuff Feinstein & Emily Shuff Klainberg**

Twins who quilt with double the stash

 Carol Goossens

Quilter and augmentative communication consultant

 Dorothea Hahn

Unrepentant fabric fanatic

 Addy Harkavy

Experimental quilter and dog mom

 Susan Horn

Wife, mother, quilter, and ice cream lover

 Sylvia Hughes

Researcher, quilter, and dog lover

 Arlene Jacobs

Professional chef and quilter

 Linda Kraynack

Sits in her room and sews all day

Diana McClun & Laura Nownes

Beloved California quilting goddesses who greatly influenced the author

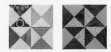

Cheryl McDaniels

The quilting archivist

Patricia McMahon

Almost retired investment advisor, almost full-time quilter

Marcella Peek

Quilting teacher and baker's apprentice

Ellen Quinn

Quilter wannabe

Jeri Riggs

Ex-psychiatrist turned fanatical quilter

Michele Shatz

She couldn't be found among her stash

Susan Stauber

Has been cutting things apart and
putting them back together since 1959

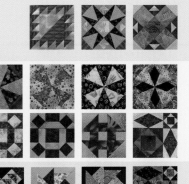

Robin Strauss

Quilter and peace activist

John Willcox

Emerging quilter

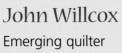

Adrienne Yorinks

Textile artist and poodle lover

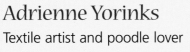

INDEX